Series Preface

D1452600

Mapping the Tradition Series

Paul Rorem, series advisor

Mapping the Tradition is a series of brief, compact guides to pivotal thinkers in Christian history. Each volume in this series focuses upon a particular figure and provides a concise but lucid introduction to the central features of each thinker's work and sketches the lasting significance of that thinker for the history of Christian theology.

As well, the series utilizes primary source works from each figure as an entry point for exposition and exploration. Guided by leading scholars in history and theology, primary source texts are reproduced with explanatory commentary, and are accompanied by orientational essays to the context, contours, and historical and conceptual legacy of the corpus.

The series is designed for beginning and intermediate students, as well as interested general readers, who will benefit from clear, helpful surveys of thinkers, texts, and theologies from across the epochs of Christian history and introduction to major issues and key historical and intellectual points of development.

Volumes in the series:

Gillian T. W. Ahlgren, *Enkindling Love: The Legacy of Teresa of Avila and John of the Cross*

Paul Rorem, *The Dionysian Mystical Tradition*

Forthcoming:

Khaled Anatolios, *Irenaeus of Lyons: The Making of the Great Tradition*

Romanus Cessario, O.P. and Cajetan Cuddy, O.P., *Thomas and the Thomists: The Achievements of Thomas Aquinas and his Interpreters*

Robert Kolb, *Luther and Christian Freedom*

Andrew Louth, *John of Damasus: The Radiance of Orthodoxy*

Paul R. Sponheim, *Existing Before God: Søren Kierkegaard and the Human Venture*

Terrence N. Tice, *Scheleiermacher: The Psychology of Christian Faith and Life*

Thomas G. Weinandy and Daniel A. Keating, *Athanasius: Trinitarian-Incarnational Soteriology and Its Reception*

Enkindling Love

Enkindling Love

The Legacy of Teresa of Avila and John of the Cross

Gillian T. W. Ahlgren

Fortress Press
Minneapolis

ENKINDLING LOVE
The Legacy of Teresa of Avila and John of the Cross

Cover design: Tory Herman

Library of Congress Cataloging-in-Publication Data
Print ISBN: 978-1-5064-0559-9
eBook ISBN: 978-1-5064-0560-5

The paper used in this publication meets the minimum requirements of American
National Standard for Information Sciences — Permanence of Paper for Printed
Library Materials, ANSI Z329.48-1984.

Manufactured in the U.S.A.

This book was produced using Pressbooks.com, and PDF rendering was done by
PrinceXML.

For Michael Joseph
with deepest gratitude and true joy

"This fire of love in you enkindles the souls of others,
and with every other virtue
you will be always awakening them..."

Teresa of Avila, *Interior Castle*, VII:4:14

God,
being God,
seeks to make us gods by participation,
just as fire
makes all things into fire.

John of the Cross, *Sayings of Light and Love*, 106

Contents

Abbreviations

AMC John of the Cross, *The Ascent of Mount Carmel*

DN   John of the Cross, *The Dark Night*

IC   Teresa of Avila, *The Interior Castle*

LF   John of the Cross, *The Living Flame of Love*

SCB John of the Cross, *The Spiritual Canticle*, Version B

L   Teresa of Avila, *The Book of Her Life*

WP   Teresa of Avila, *The Way of Perfection*

I have prepared new translations for all of the textual passages in this volume. I have relied on these critical editions in Spanish:

TOC   Teresa de Avila, *Obras completas*, ed. Alberto Barrientos et al., Madrid: Editorial de Espiritualidad, 1984.

JOC   Juan de la Cruz, *Obras completas*, ed. Lucinio Ruano de la Iglesia, Madrid: BAC, 1982.

CWJC *The Collected Works of St. John of the Cross* translated by Kieran Kavanaugh and Otilio Rodriguez. Washington, DC: Institute of Carmelite Studies, 1979.

CWTA *The Collected Works of St. Teresa of Avila* 3 vols., translated by Kieran Kavanaugh and Otilio Rodríguez. Washington, DC: Institute of Carmelite Studies, 1980.

Preface

Teresa of Avila (1515–82) and John of the Cross (1542–91) are two of Christianity's greatest mystical theologians and spiritual teachers. Through their lives and writings, even from a distance of 500 years, we gain a unique glimpse of God. The legacy of these two impressive figures is that they introduce us to a God who is unfathomably generous and who longs for us with a heartbreaking fidelity and patience. This is a God who draws us into the work of making the world a place where everyone belongs, is cherished, and is accorded the innate dignity given to each human person. Their God is keenly interested in us and "constantly gazing at us," with eyes that "anticipate, radiate, penetrate and elicit beauty."[1] Their legacy is as keenly relevant to our day as it was to the time of great change and reform to which they belonged.

To appreciate Teresa and John in their totality, as teachers, writers, theologians, spiritual directors, religious reformers, and human beings, is a massive undertaking. Between the two of them, they wrote eight major works, many minor works, poetry, and literally thousands of notes, counsels, and letters. This outpouring of written material is but a small echo of the creative abundance of God in their lives. Their spiritual-theological synthesis represents one of the great achievements of the Christian mystical tradition, and when one understands this synthesis within its historical context, the two

---

1. Iain Matthew, *Impact of God* (London: Hodder and Stoughton, 1995), 28.

emerge as people worthy of our most profound admiration for what they accomplished as human beings.

There are obvious limitations to the kind of introduction to them that we can give in this short volume. And yet, their message is so fundamental and critical that it seems important to move surgically to the heart of what they have to offer. I shall try very hard to do that, and to do so, I will often relegate interesting and important themes to footnotes and send readers to the massive bibliography that their writings have also spawned. If I accomplish anything in this volume, I hope to give readers an introduction both to the content and substance of their theological contributions to the tradition and an invitation, at the human level, to the transformative energy that their writings convey.

Teresa and John wrote, primarily, to help others. Each had personally experienced God as a revolutionary source of vitality, capable of changing literally everything. As they dedicated themselves to partnership with God, they were determined to facilitate others' direct access to the God who had so transformed their lives. They were compassionate and dedicated contemplative teachers; they wrote for their companions on the way, knowing from experience where they might struggle, anticipating their needs, providing encouragement, and explaining how to continue on. They used simple yet evocative language, constantly self-critical, always pushing themselves to find words for the experiences that had left them thoroughly undone—"lost" on a path without words and "found" in ways they could not contain for themselves alone.

Teresa and John wrote because they had to—not (as so many commentators continue to say about Teresa) out of obedience; not only to try to communicate all that they had discovered about God; not only to extend to others, by imitation, the loving invitation to relationship that God had extended to them—but because they were now afire with a love that wanted to burn its way into the hearts of people they could not accompany in person. For them, not to write would be to try to hold back, within oneself (as if one could), the flooding dams of a wide river needing to spill out and make its course across the earth. Not to write would be an act of disdain, ingratitude, and utter infidelity to the invitation of their Beloved to share generously the love that they themselves had been graced and privileged to receive. Not to write would be to refuse to sing of the joyful partnership with God toward which the whole of their being was attuned.

Teresa and John's thorough dedication to "this process of finding words for that for which there are no words," as Joan Chittister defines "incarnation," is a testimony to the process of incarnation itself and all of the patient midwifery that it involves. For Teresa, to lose an insight by letting it die—that is, by not putting it into action or sharing it with the one to whom she thought it might help—was an infidelity worthy of immediately seeking out her confessor.[2] It was this kind of purity of conscience that motivated her and gradually wrote its way out by candlelight, as she plowed through correspondence late at night or stayed faithful to the writing of the *Interior Castle* around administrative duties that might have kept any author today from setting pen to paper.[3] John, too, wrote because people sought his spiritual counsel, which he spontaneously and generously gave as often as he could, but then also realized that his spiritual counsel was only as valuable as the time and space people had to take it in. Reading and re-reading a letter, an "aviso," a poem written in a moment of contemplative union would support even more deeply the spiritual progress of those he was committed to accompanying. This instinct to help, to explain, to console, and to encourage was what gave rise to his mystical treatises.

Although we today might initially turn to Teresa and John (just as their own contemporaries did) as guides who can help us find our way, Iain Matthew identifies John's greatest gift as the capacity "not so much to tell us what to do, how to pinpoint our place on the map,

---

2. See, for example, Teresa, letter 133 to Jerónimo Gracián (23 October 1576) and letter 162, also to Gracián (18 December 1576).

3. For insight into what the writing process was like for Teresa, see Ahlgren, *Teresa of Avila and the Politics of Sanctity* (*TAPS*) (Ithaca, NY: Cornell University, 1996), 68–84, esp. the testimony of eyewitness María del Nacimiento, 78.

but to draw back the curtains and disclose the whole journey as real."[4] I think this simple sentence captures well the core of what Teresa and John offer us: even today, they help us to discern the presence of God in our lives. They help us to recognize and cling to what is most real, what matters most. We turn to them as spiritual teachers and end up being drawn into the grace at work in our own lives and the joy of collaborating in something far greater than ourselves. We read them and end up engaging theology through the back door. Or, we come clean and do the kind of theology that changes lives (ours and others'), instead of skittering at the edges of what really matters.

It is not easy to sift through outpourings of material, written by two highly intelligent, keenly sensitive human beings, both absolutely committed to leaving behind all that was not God in order to live in the depths of partnership that the mystical life entails. I shall maintain focus by trying to pinpoint what they would say if they could speak only once.[5] This leads me to privilege Teresa's more mature *Interior Castle* over her *Life*, both because of its more systematic coherence and because it integrates insights (theological, spiritual, and psychological) that were not possible for her to articulate in her earlier works. It also draws me to move directly to specific parts of John's mystical corpus that facilitate a telescopic view of transforming relationship with God. And in footnotes, I have indicated some of the resonances between the stages in the mystical life as the two of them outline them.

Although the emphasis I am giving to the "testimonial" function of their works may suggest that I see them primarily as spiritual guides teaching out of their experience of God, that is not actually my primary concern. I spent a good part of my early career trying to ensure proper

---

4. Matthew, *Impact of God*, 16.
5. I derive this helpful principle from *Impact of God*, 3, where Matthew describes his method: "We shall go in stages. One step will be to find John's most personal word about God, what he would say if he could speak only once." For that insight, as well as for inspiration, friendship and just plain pure genius, I would like to express my debt to Iain. *Enkindling Love* took shape around not one, but two international congresses on the impact of Teresa of Avila on the occasion of the 500th anniversary of her birth, during which time, we met and began to forge a prayerful friendship. Each time that I would feel discouraged at the challenge of communicating and bringing to life the profound legacy of Teresa and John, I would pick up Iain's extraordinary and masterful *The Impact of God: Soundings from St. John of the Cross*, know that he was praying for me across a wide expanse of ocean, and quickly gain the strength to keep plowing forward.

appreciation of their work as theologians—an effort that, at this point, no longer seems as necessary as it once was. But if we do now understand Teresa and John as theologians, this truly begs several questions: (1) Who do they invite us to come to know, and how does their God challenge and surprise us, even as we find this God imminently recognizable both in Scripture and tradition? (2) How does their deep dedication to intimacy with God inform our understanding of what theology itself is? (3) What are the qualifications for theological inquiry and authority? Can one really be a theologian without some rigorous relational experience of God? And how would we gauge that authenticity today? I could not possibly hope to answer those questions. But it is my hope that readers of this volume would begin to pose them because of the rich synthesis that these two authors offer us.

While *Enkindling Love* fits beautifully into Fortress' new Mapping the Tradition series, its gestation has been long. The manuscript contains threaded scraps of conversations that extend back to 2007, when I first started taking notes on John, and the project, as a whole, gained energy from exchanges at the many congresses on Teresa held in 2015, the 500th anniversary of her birth. It would be impossible to name all of the people whose comments, conversation, critical feedback, translation consultation, and general support made this book possible, but, among others, I would like to mention: Sarah Coakley, Eddie Howells, José María Mantero, Iain Matthew, Bernard and Patricia McGinn, Nohemi Melgarejo, Colin Thompson, Peter Tyler, and all who worked to make 2015 a year that truly honored the spirit of Teresa de Jesús. Some of my recent work on John of the Cross—still unpublished, but helpful in the preparation of this book—was supported by a Sabbatical Grant for Researchers from the Louisville Institute. I am also grateful for support from the Spanish Ministry of Culture's Program for Cultural Cooperation.

My warmest thanks, however, are reserved for the one whose hospitality planted the seeds of this book eight years ago. Sitting in the corner of his garden next to fragrant shoots of phlox, a gentle breeze drew tender tears from both of my eyes, and I was moved in a heartbeat to the space of "dejando mi cuidado entre las azucenas olividado." As I turned to thank him, he handed me his cherished volume of John of the Cross, and invited me back to life. It is friendships such as this one that transform our dark nights of struggle and angst into loving encounters full of tender possibility. And for this friendship, I am most grateful—Deo gratias.

1

Introduction

In order to understand the boldness of Teresa and John's spiritual and theological synthesis, we must locate them in the "harsh times"[1] in which they lived. As I have attempted to articulate in other places,[2] the spirituality of sixteenth-century Spain is a complex chimera. For about 100 years, beginning around 1525, the Spanish Inquisition's suspicion of interiority and "mental prayer" resulted in ongoing investigation and punishment of *alumbrados* (a pejorative term meaning, effectively, those who have been "falsely illumined"),[3] as well as intense scrutiny—and even censorship—of spiritual works, many of which ended up on the Spanish Indices of Prohibited Books.[4] Such a climate

---

1. See L 33:5, where Teresa describes concerns articulated by her friends and neighbors in Avila, right at the moment of her first reformed convent (1562): "And then the devil began to try to stir things up through one person and another by having them understand that I had seen some kind of revelation in this business, and they came to me with a lot of fear, telling me that these were harsh times ["tiempos recios"] and that perhaps people would rise up against me and go to the inquisitors . . ."
2. See Ahlgren, *TAPS*, 6–31; see also Gillian T. W. Ahlgren, *Entering Teresa of Avila's Interior Castle: A Reader's Companion*, 5–18; and Ahlgren, "Negotiating Sanctity: Holy Women in Sixteenth-Century Spain," *Church History* vol. 64, no. 3 (September, 1995): 373–88.
3. For more on the impact of Inquisitional suspicion of *alumbrados* on Teresa, see *TAPS*, 9–15 and *Entering*, pp. 1–13; for more on the *alumbrados* themselves, see Alastair Hamilton, *Heresy and Mysticism in Sixteenth-Century Spain* (James Clarke and Co., 1992).
4. The two major Indexes of Prohibited Books in sixteenth-century Spain were the Valdés Index (1559) and the Quiroga Index (1583). As I argued in *TAPS*, 32–66, the Valdés Index had a particular

created a minefield for people who, like Teresa and John, sensed the whisper of God to deeper relationship with God and deeper personal authenticity. It is deeply ironic that one of the most inhospitable spaces for spiritual depth produced some of Christianity's greatest mystics and spiritual teachers.

But Spanish religious officials had not always been suspicious of spirituality and mental prayer. In fact, religious reforms grounded in monastic reforms, humanist education, biblical study, and new translations of classics from the medieval mystical tradition were part of the reforms supported by Catholic monarchs Ferdinand and Isabel, beginning in the 1480s. At the time of Teresa's birth in 1515, Spanish humanism was at its height. Under the leadership of Cardinal Francisco Jiménez de Cisneros, confessor to Queen Isabella, and with the help of the humanist press at the University of Alcalá, a major spiritual reform was inaugurated. This reform movement had, at its center, vernacular translations of major medieval treatises on contemplative prayer and the mystical life, including texts by Augustine, Gregory the Great, Cassian, Bernard of Clairvaux, John Climacus, Angela of Foligno, and Hugh of Balma, whose *Sol de contemplativos* made accessible the affective Dionysian tradition developed by the Victorine school and sixteenth-century Spanish Franciscan writers such as Francisco de Osuna and Bernardino de Laredo.[5]

This intense commitment to developing a vernacular spirituality

---

impact on Teresa: as her understanding of the need for authoritative books on contemplative prayer in the vernacular increased, she was moved "from reading books to writing them." See *Ibid.*, esp. 39–41. For more on the impact of Inquisitional censorship in sixteenth-century Spain, see Virgilio Pinto Crespo, *Inquisición y control ideológico en la España del siglo XVI* (Barcelona: Ariel, 1983).

5. For a review of Spanish schools of spirituality in the late fifteenth century and early sixteenth century, including Cisneros' influence, see Melquíades Andres, *La teología española en el siglo XVI* 2 vols. (Madrid: Biblioteca de Autores Cristianos, 1976) I:356–426. For a list of medieval treatises available in the vernacular in the early sixteenth century, see *Ibid.*, 378–90. I summarize Cisneros' influence briefly, noting the shift toward growing suspicion of interiority after 1525, in *TAPS*, 9–15. On Hugh of Balma and the development of affective Dionysianism in Spain, see Peter Tyler, *The Return to the Mystical: Ludwig Wittgenstein, Teresa of Avila, and the Christian Mystical Tradition* (New York: Continuum, 2011). See also the text in translation in *Carthusian Spirituality: The Writings of Hugh of Balma and Guigo de Ponte* trans. Dennis D. Martin (Mahwah, NY: Paulist Press, 1997), with attention to Martin's introductory comments on affective prayer and the "taming" of Pseudo-Dionysius in *Ibid.*, 35–40. On Francisco de Osuna and Bernardino de Laredo, see Tyler, *Return to the Mystical*, 112–23 and 124–30, respectively; see also the Classics of Western Spirituality translation of Francisco de Osuna's *Spiritual Alphabet* (Mahwah, NJ: Paulist Press, 1981).

rooted in a thorough harvesting of medieval mystical treatises made it possible for an "unlettered" woman[6] such as Teresa to pursue what was, at first, an intensely personal quest to understand her lived experience of God. However, as she dedicated herself to the contemplative life, shared her thirst with others, received as much training and spiritual counsel as she could, and engaged a reform of her religious order, Teresa became, herself, a leading figure in Spanish spirituality and even developed a sophisticated theological synthesis,[7] despite opposition from some of her contemporaries, who would have preferred that she kept silent. Her fruitful collaboration with John of the Cross in the reform of the order, beginning in 1567, stimulated both of them to realize their vocation to the mystical life and to articulate and share with their contemporaries their insights about God's profoundly mysterious and liberating accessibility.

Because of their popularity, the details of Teresa and John's life have been painstakingly studied, and there is a rich bibliography to provide the biographical detail that I cannot include here.[8] They were brought up in very different environments, although they have very similar genealogical profiles. Born in 1515, Teresa was raised in a blended family of twelve children, two by her father's first marriage. "We were three sisters and nine brothers," she writes in her *Life*.[9] She lost her

---

6. To Teresa and her contemporaries, "unlettered" people were those who could not read Latin. In this sense, Teresa, like most women and, indeed, most men outside the church, was unlettered. This, in no way, should fool us into thinking that she was uneducated. As I have argued elsewhere, Teresa's theological education rivaled that of many of her male colleagues. (See, for example, Ahlgren, *TAPS*, 39: "Despite her inability to read Latin and her lack of training in the scholastic method of the universities, Teresa had certainly read as much as many of her better versed confessors, perhaps more. . . . Lacking a teacher of contemplative technique, Teresa actively searched for guidance in contemporary spiritual literature.")

7. I summarize that synthesis briefly in Ahlgren, "Teresa of Avila" in Carter Lindberg, ed., *The Reformation Theologians* (Oxford: Blackwell, 2002), 311–24.

8. For starters on Teresa, I recommend my *TAPS*; Barbara Mujica, *Teresa of Ávila: Lettered Woman*; Peter Tyler, *Teresa of Avila: Doctor of the Soul* (London: Bloomsbury, 2013); Alison Weber, *Teresa of Avila and the Rhetoric of Femininity* (Princeton: Princeton University Press, 1991), and for Spanish-speakers, Daniel de Pablo Maroto, *Santa Teresa de Jesús: Nueva biografía (Escritora, fundadora, maestro)* (Madrid: Editorial de Espiritualidad, 2014). On John of the Cross, see Leonard Doohan, *The Contemporary Challenge of John of the Cross: An Introduction to His Life and Teaching* (Washington, DC: Institute of Carmelite Studies, 1995); Kieran Kavanaugh. *John of the Cross: Doctor of Light and Love*. New York: Crossroad, 1999; Matthew, *Impact of God*; Colin Thompson, *John of the Cross: Songs in the Night* (Washington, DC: Catholic University of America Press, 2003); and Peter M. Tyler, *St. John of the Cross* (New York: Continuum, 2010).

9. L 1:4.

mother when she was twelve years old, and shortly after that, she was sent to live at the school associated with a local Augustinian convent. Teresa's father was a prosperous merchant, but the family's lack of "pure blood" (Teresa's paternal grandfather had converted to Christianity from Judaism and was prosecuted by the Spanish Inquisition) kept them from full integration, either into old Spanish society or into careers of public service.[10] Nearly all of her nine brothers emigrated to the Americas, seeking fame and fortune—and indeed, it was the money they acquired there that would later enable Teresa to begin her reform movement.[11] John was born in 1542, the youngest of three children born to Gonzalo de Yepes, from a wealthy family of silk merchants in Toledo with *converso* origins. When Gonzalo married Catalina Alvarez, from a family of weavers in Medina del Campo (who may herself have been a daughter of *moriscos*, or Muslims continuing to live in Spain as a separate ethnic group), he was disowned. Gonzalo died when John was three years old, and the family struggled to survive. John's older brother Luis died when John was just eight years old—effectively, of poverty. John found refuge in a school for orphans, and then, when he was 17, he began to work at Nuestra Señora de la Concepción, a hospital established to serve those suffering from incurable diseases. Ironically, many of his patients languished of syphilis, a new disease that had entered Spain with the return of conquistadores from the Americas. John attended the Jesuit College in Medina del Campo during the years 1559-63, which would have given him a strong general grounding in the humanities—specifically, grammar, rhetoric, Greek and Latin, with exposure to Jerome, Aquinas, Bonaventure, and other theological writers.

Both Teresa and John seemed to have joined the Carmelites almost by default, although it is noteworthy that it was one of the few religious

---

10. Sixteenth-century Spain was marked by concern over "limpieza de sangre," or purity of lineage, and there were statutes in place to keep families of Jewish origin from public office, and even, from entering many religious orders. On the impact of the statutes, see Albert A. Sicroff, *Los Estatutos de Limpieza de Sangre: controversias entre los siglos XV y XVII* (Madrid: Taurus, 1985).

11. Hernando, Rodrigo, Lorenzo, Antonio, Jerónimo, Agustín, and Pedro, all went to the Americas. Lorenzo was responsible for the money that went to purchase the house that became San José in Avila, and he contributed more to the reform upon his return to Spain in the 1570s. For a detailed summary of Teresa's brothers' lives as *conquistadores* see Maroto, *Santa Teresa de Jesús*, 65-71.

orders in sixteenth-century Spain that resisted cultural and social discrimination against people of *converso* origin.[12] Teresa entered the convent of the Encarnación in November 1535 and spent 27 years there, before leaving to found the reformed convent of San José in Avila in 1562. John joined the Carmelite order in 1563, and then went on to study theology at the College of San Andrés in Salamanca. In 1567, he was ordained a priest and returned to Medina del Campo, where he and Teresa crossed paths for the first time.

But before we review the full flowering of their collaboration, it will be helpful to mention briefly the work of Teresa, which had cleared the path for a new mystical way. The drama of Teresa's early religious life, especially as she recounts it in her *Life*, is well-known: her severe illness as a young woman, which led her to dedicate herself to the study and practice of prayer (1535–42)[13]; her struggles to find adequate spiritual direction (1542–54)[14]; her gradual conversion to deepening friendship with Christ, culminating at the point in which she says, "from here onward, it is a whole new life . . . one that God lives in me" (1554–59)[15]; the stabilizing influence of Jesuit spiritual direction and Ignatian meditative practice[16]; increasing controversy as her prayer life grew more intense[17]; the growing desire for a lifestyle and monastic context that would support her deepening relationship with God[18]; a

12. The Carmelites held off adopting the Statutes of Limpieza de Sangre until after Teresa's death, and the Jesuits resisted until 1593. By contrast, the Dominicans adopted the Statutes in 1489, the Hieronymites in 1493, and the Franciscans in 1525.

13. See L chapters 4–6. Teresa's initial spiritual formation, particularly as it was mediated by the engagement with Jerome's letters, Gregory the Great's *Moralia*, John Cassian's *Conferences*, and other basics began during this timeframe.

14. L chapters 7–8 and 23.

15. This period would include the famous Lenten meditation before a statue of Christ during the Passion (the flagellation or an Ecce Homo) described in chapter 9 of the *Life* as well as experiences of the presence of Christ that helped her separate her life into a "before" and "after"—a period that Daniel de Pablo Maroto calls her "dark night" and which he dates from 1554 through 1559. See discussion in Maroto, 148–61, esp. 157 for his mention of the "dark night." Teresa's clarity about the "new life" granted to her after this time is expressed in L 23:1: "It is a whole new book from here on forward—I mean, a whole new life. The one up to here was mine. The one that I have lived since I began to speak of these prayer experiences is the one that God is living in me, or so it seems to me." Cf. Galatians 2:20.

16. See L, chapter 24.

17. See L, chapter 25.

18. The Carmelite convent of the Encarnación in Avila housed over 150 sisters and could not afford to feed and support all of them. Women of means were encouraged to leave the convent and eat with their families. Teresa herself, a popular and vivacious woman, was encouraged to cultivate

yearning for consistency, authenticity, and integration in her own life; and a communal space in which the true *communio* of the mystical life could be sustained. All of this turbulence bore fruit in the foundation of the first Discalced Carmelite convent of San José in 1562 and in the freedom, to create and sustain, with God and others, the unitive life to which Teresa felt called.

As Teresa herself reflected on these years of turbulence and contradiction, she recognized the hand of God in them, weaning her gently of all other authorities (whether confessors, spiritual directors, or even spiritual books), so that she could learn directly from God, the fount of all wisdom: "It seems to me now that God provided where I could not find anyone to teach me . . ."[19] And this perspective seems to mirror John of the Cross' description of the process of the dark night of the spirit, where the soul is weaned of derivative experiences of God (as helpful as they may have been to the soul in its earliest stages of spiritual growth), so that God can begin to instruct the soul directly. Both Teresa and John retained strong concerns about spiritual directors and other "experts" hampering the direct communication of God and the soul, and these concerns were surely rooted in the lack of spiritual depth and experience of most of their contemporaries. In Teresa's case, these concerns (and the strong memories of her own vulnerability in the hands of those who should have exhibited better pastoral skill and spiritual wisdom) instilled in her a resolve to protect others from the kind of pernicious doubt and second-guessing of God's grace and generosity that she had so often experienced because of the doubt of her confessors and guides.[20] Teresa's sincere lament over the

friendships with potential donors to the community and found her dedication to contemplative prayer often disrupted by visits, conversations, and other consultations. See L 32:9: "This habit of leaving the house, even though I was one who used it often, was very inconvenient for me, because some people, whom the prelates could not refuse, liked me to be in their company, and so they would ask them to order me to go to them; and thus, as I was ordered, I was only rarely able to actually be in the convent." Teresa turned this situation into an occasion to meet with spiritual teachers and, gradually, to gather a vision and support for a new form of contemplative life. As Daniel Pablo de Maroto chronicles, Teresa was absent from the convent from 1555 to 1558, living in the house of Guiomar de Ulloa; again in 1559 to consult with Pedro de Alcántara and Maridíaz; and then again, toward the end of 1561 until June 1562, in the house of Luisa de la Cerda in Toledo. See Maroto, 145–47.

19. L 4:9.

20. See especially L 29:5–7, where Teresa describes the "great distress" caused by having to make a

appearance of the Valdés Index of Prohibited Books in 1559 and her subsequent vocation as a spiritual teacher and writer of mystical texts was also born out of this tremendously conflictive time, as she records:

> When they took away many books written in the vernacular so that they would not be read, I felt this keenly, because reading some of them gave me solace, and now I could not read them, since they were in Latin. But then God said to me, "Do not be sad; I will give you a living book." I could not understand why this was said to me . . . but then only a few days later, I understood it quite well . . . , for [since then] God has favored me with so much love as to teach me in so many ways that I have had little or even no need for books.[21]

Readers of Teresa's *Life* end up feeling a vicarious sense of relief as Teresa's struggles for spiritual authenticity resolve themselves within the context of her reform movement. While it would be naïve to idealize the religious houses or the women and men who lived in them, it is worth recognizing that both Teresa and John committed themselves intensely to the life-with-God that could be explored in that context and to the pastoral care of all those who entered them. They were intelligent people, eminently practical, and, at least in John's case, quite gentle, and in 1567, when they joined forces in the reform, a new experiment in holiness began.

When Teresa and John met for the first time in Medina del Campo, Teresa was finalizing the foundation of the second reformed convent of the Discalced Carmelite order and just beginning to imagine more of the small contemplative communities that her new constitutions called for.[22] In particular, she wanted a community of men to be part of the reform, especially because then, she and her sisters would have

---

sign of contempt toward Christ, out of obedience to confessors who had ordered her to do so whenever she felt Christ present. Daniel de Pablo Maroto draws connections between some of Teresa's physical illnesses and the stress that these conflicts over authority caused in her. See Maroto, *Santa Teresa de Jesús*, 138–41.

21. L 26:5; see discussion in *TAPS*, 39–42.

22. For a review of Teresa's vision and the history of the Constitutions that governed the reform, see Alison Weber, "Spiritual Administration: Gender and Discernment in the Carmelite Reform" in *Sixteenth-Century Studies* 31(1) Spring 2000:123–46. See also Otger Steggink, "Arraigo carmelitano de Santa Teresa," in *The Land of Carmel: Essays in Honor of Joachim Smet*, ed. Paul Chandler and Keith J. Egan (Rome: Institutum Carmelitanum, 1991), 259–84, and Daniel de Pablo Maroto, *Ser y misión del Carmelo Teresiano: Historia de un carisma* (Madrid: Editorial de Espiritualidad, 2010).

priests and confessors who were themselves well-formed in the mystical life. John sought greater solitude than the Carmelite tradition was offering him and was considering a transfer to the Carthusian order. Although the two were of very different temperaments, it did not take them long to recognize their similar vision, passion, determination, and longing. It was an intense yearning to bring the searing love of God into the world, and Teresa immortalizes their joint passion to endure anything for the love of God in a throwaway comment in the sixth dwelling places of her *Interior Castle*, when she writes:

> I know of someone—well, of two people, one of whom was a man—to whom God had given some of these favors . . . and yet, they so yearned to suffer that they complained to our Lord because God was giving them such great gifts, and if they could refuse to receive them, they would.[23]

John initially installed himself in a very primitive house at Duruelo, where he and up to three others lived a legendary life of poverty and austerity that suited a fierce depth of interior prayer. Teresa describes how their prayer was so deep that during the harsh days of winter, snow would gather on their habits without their even noticing.[24]

Several years later, beginning in 1571, their collaborative energy bore its deepest fruit when Teresa was appointed prioress of the large (and still unreformed) convent of the Encarnación. Very aware of the convent's dynamics, Teresa took on the task with trepidation. One of her first decisions was to bring the kindly, wise John, not yet thirty years old, to serve as the convent's spiritual director. As she wrote of him later to another sister, this "celestial and divine man . . . is without equal in all of Castile. There is no one who inspires such fervor on the path to heaven."[25] Teresa was certain that John's care and spiritual encouragement of the sisters at the Encarnación would inspire greater thirst for and commitment to the mystical life. The move was a brilliant one. As Teresa well knew, "you cannot begin to recollect yourselves by

---

23. M VI:9:17.
24. F 13–14, especially her description in 14:6–12. See discussion in Tyler, *St. John of the Cross*, 21–22.
25. From Letter 268, November 1578.

force but only by gentleness, if your recollection is going to be more continual."[26] As one of the sisters at the Encarnación later recalled of John, "He had a gift for consoling those who came to him, by his words and in the cards he wrote . . . I received some myself—also some jottings about spiritual matters. I would dearly love to have them now."[27]

This time period of the mid-1570s at the Encarnación represents one of the tradition's greatest and most deliberate collaborations between two great mystics. Their success in establishing Avila as a dynamic space of dedication to the mystical life triggered substantial resistance to the reform, even as the nuns at the Encarnación made great progress through the first half of the 1570s.[28] For Teresa, too, these were years of significant growth in the mystical life. Insights that she could not yet articulate when she wrote *The Book of Her Life* were becoming clearer and more comprehensible as her unitive life with God grew more integrated and sustained. It was precisely in the years between 1572 and 1577 that, experientially, she entered into the realms of the mystical life that she would soon describe as the seven dwelling places of the *Interior Castle*. In this culmination of the unitive life, Teresa no longer knew God only in partial encounters, but continually lived in the constancy of a realized partnership with God, participating in the Trinitarian life. Teresa's capacity to articulate these experiences is reflected in the *Interior Castle*, written in 1577 and superseding, theologically, her *Life*.

What happens next in the chronology (we are in November 1577—literally three days after Teresa finished writing her *Interior Castle*) is both a travesty and a sort of watershed for the entire mystical tradition. John of the Cross was violently kidnapped by his nonreformed brothers in religious life. Taken from Avila to Toledo,

---

26. IC II:1:10; see below, pp. 27–8.
27. Silverio de Santa Teresa, ed., *Biblioteca Mística Carmelitana* 10:31, cited in Matthew, *Impact of God*, 19–20.
28. We will review the resistance to Teresa and John below. See Leonard Doohan's brief summary of this "golden age" in his *The Contemporary Challenge of John of the Cross: An Introduction to His Life and Teaching*, p. 13: "Eventually John became, along with Teresa, one of the two principal spiritual guides of the Incarnation, and by the end of 1572 peace and renewal were coming to the convent. . . . While at the Incarnation, John's reputation as a spiritual guide grew, and others outside the convent entrusted extremely difficult discernment cases to him."

he spent nine months in captivity, where flogging and severe mental torture turned his world inside out. As he referred to the experience a few years later to Catalina de Jesús, "that whale swallowed me up and vomited me out."[29] Peter Tyler is right to call this "an iconic nine months . . . the transforming moment of his life."[30] The fact that he survived is remarkable enough; that this experience somehow helped crystallize for him the reality of God's tenderness and loving care is testimony both to his maturity as a human being and to something core, essential, and powerful about the ontological bond between God and humanity.

Teresa responded to John's kidnapping with shock, horror, and direct advocacy. She immediately did everything she could to locate and rescue him, appealing to religious and secular authorities to intervene in a situation that cried out for adjudication and remediation. More privately, in a letter to María de San José, prioress of the Discalced convent in Seville, Teresa revealed not only her indignation at the injustice of the events, but her personal sorrow and distress, feeling deeply the specific details: John and his companion Germán de San Matías had been lashed several times and violently treated; when Germán was taken away, the sisters of the Encarnación said that he was bleeding through his mouth.[31] Teresa begged María de San José for her prayers, both for her sisters and for the two "holy prisoners," and her language indicates that she is keenly aware of the suffering of her friends. In her ongoing correspondence with María over the next months, she keeps vigil, marking time from the day that they were seized: "Tomorrow will make eight days that they have been imprisoned . . . " and, "For although today makes sixteen days since our two brothers were imprisoned, we do not know if they have released them . . . "[32] For the next six months, Teresa used all means possible to advocate for the release of John of the Cross, considering who might be able to influence, compel, and/or punish the Calced who

---

29. John of the Cross, Letter to Catalina de Jesús from Baeza, dated July 6, 1581. JOC, 874.
30. See Tyler, St. John of the Cross, 27.
31. Letter 214: 9 (December 10, 1577).
32. Letter 214:10; Letter 215:2.

had imprisoned him. Her letters during this time reflect her efforts to secure intervention, from state and ecclesiastical officials, that would provide for John of the Cross' liberation and for the protection of the Discalced from the governance of the Calced.[33] Despite her efforts, John remained imprisoned until he himself escaped from the Calced brothers in Toledo in August 1578, nine months after being seized from his home. When she learned of his treatment in more detail, Teresa expressed her shock and abhorrence of the injustice in a letter to Jerónimo Gracián, encouraging him to inform the papal nuncio of the entire situation.[34] Here, we see both Teresa's righteous indignation and her conviction that bringing darkness and injustice into the light is a service both to God and to God's people. Teresa's actions provide a clear example of the prophetic dimensions of contemplative life.

Both the "Dark Night" and the "Spiritual Canticle" were born in this pitiful moment of John's life, although it would take months for him to recover, physically and emotionally, from the experience,[35] and only in subsequent years could the poetry and its commentary make their way to writing. Although his spirituality is often characterized with words like "passivity" and even "quietism", it should be instructive to us that he courageously and stealthily found the means to escape from captivity. This would have required him to unbolt the padlocked door, measure the distance from the monastery window down the cliffs to the city wall below, fashion a sturdy enough rope from strips of his blanket and what remained of his clothing, get down the rope under cover of night, and make his way painfully to the discalced convent across town.[36]

---

33. See, for example, her letter to Teutonio de Braganza of January 16, 1578, which mentions a formal complaint to the Consejo (Letter 217:12). See also her correspondence with Roque de Huerta in Madrid (dated March 9, 1578) and her letter to Jerónimo Gracián dated March 10–11, 1578.

34. Letter 252 (August 21, 1578): "I tell you that it really weighs on me what they have done to friar John of the Cross; I do not know how God permits such things. . . . Through all these nine months past he was in a cell in which he hardly even fit, as small as he is, and in all that time he could not even change his tunic, even though he was at the point of death. . . . It is good that the details be known, that people might be on their guard against such folk. May God forgive them!"

35. All contemporary sources record John as slight and not terribly robust; this leads Peter Tyler to speculate that the nine months of grueling conditions in the cell "probably contributed significantly to his early death at 49 in 1591." See Tyler, *St. John of the Cross*, 27.

36. Peter Tyler reconstructs this in Tyler, *St. John of the Cross*, 27–28, 32.

Teresa and John spoke of God with power and authority. People who listened deeply to what they taught were changed. The fact that their teachings generated strong, even violent, resistance from some who rejected the reforms they called for is, likely, another indication of both the authenticity of their message and how compelling their understanding of God and of the mystical life was. The depth and substance of their teaching, its subjective richness, and its capacity to resonate with readers across time and space give us new eyes to understand our own reality. Over the 25 years that I have been teaching this material, it is a source of encouragement and consolation to me to see how it creates possibilities for generations of people to gain insight into their own lived experience of God.

In a culture that is as superficial as ours so often is[37], Teresa and John not only invite us to the depth and richness of life, but also "help people connect with the vitality concealed in what is already there."[38] If today's "shortage of depth" is intellectual, moral, and spiritual, it is also, simply, human. Indeed, there is a general confusion of what it is to be human, of what truly matters, of how to live a meaningful life despite the chaos of an age in which there is simply too much information, too much data to sort through. This makes an insight such as John's simple—"it was for this goal of love that we were created,"[39] a vital truth that has the capacity to pierce the blur of our daily lives with the kind of light that brings hope and the possibility of change.

What Teresa and John make clear to us is that we are, each of us, created for union with God. Nothing less than that will satisfy us. We yearn for lives that make sense in the light of love, and, as so many

37. At an international conference entitled "Networking Jesuit Higher Education: Shaping the Future for a Humane, Just, Sustainable Globe," held in Mexico City April 22–24, 2010, superior general of the Jesuits Adolfo Nicolás spoke compellingly of the "globalization of superficiality" that is endemic to our information age. His address, "Depth, Universality, and Learned Ministry: Challenges to Jesuit Higher Education Today," is available in the *Santa Clara Magazine* at http://www.scu.edu/scm/winter2010/shapingthefuture.cfm.

38. See Matthew, *Impact of God*, 17: "John lived in an age which was well-fed with religiosity. There was no shortage of religious material, but John did perceive a shortage of depth. His concern is not to add to the material, but to help people connect with the vitality concealed in what is already there."

39. *SCB* 29:3: "Since God has solemnly entreated that no one awaken a soul from this love [cf. Song of Songs 3:5], who will dare to do so and remain without reproof? After all, this love is the end for which we were created."

of Christianity's great mystics have taught, we cannot be satisfied by anything less than God. What is more (and what is even more amazing) is that this powerful longing within us is only the smallest echo of a far deeper longing, in God, for us. As Iain Matthew puts it, so beautifully, as he describes John's work "pulses with God's eagerness to belong to other persons."[40] Teresa and John teach us God's deep generosity, God's constant self-giving; they show us "a self-communicating God, a God whose plan is to fill us with nothing less than God." Indeed, as Iain Matthew writes, "John's universe is drenched in a self-outpouring God."[41]

This is not always how John has been understood. In fact, his prose seems studded with austerity, and many would point to how often John counsels readers to aspire to, literally, "nada" (nothing). John wants us to cultivate our desire to cling to nothing in life other than God. But rather than being stark, John's "nada" is not really "nothing." Instead, it is an ample relational space, as "nada" replaces the smallness of the self with the fullness that union with God brings. But in order to reach such complete union, the desire for the unitive life must take full sway in a person's life. Our high destiny, according to John, is the aspiration to "a love equal to God's." Indeed, we have "always desired this equality, naturally and supernaturally, for lovers cannot be satisfied if they fail to feel that they love as much as they are loved."[42] As our experience of God's love intensifies, so does our desire for full consummation of this love—a goal which would seem impossible if that loving desire were not the very seed of God planted within us. As Teresa and John both teach, the image of God, if we dedicate ourselves to cultivating it, will burn its way through our being until, we too, are part of the living flame of love that fires all life.

In an age in which people are weary and even jaded, dubious, and hesitant to invest themselves in anything, Teresa and John's confidence in the power of desire, rightly ordered and intensely focused, can provide a hopeful and helpful path toward joy and

40. Matthew, *Impact of God*, 25.
41. Ibid.
42. *SCB* 38:3.

fulfillment. Rather than cutting off desire and clipping our wings, Teresa and John teach us that love asks us to soar higher than we could hope. As Iain Matthew writes:

> Survival demands a certain skepticism. We are trained to cope as social beings by keeping our desires within realistic limits. But where God is concerned, the problem lies in our desiring too little, and growing means expanding our expectations; or rather, making God's generosity, not our poverty, the measure of our expectations.[43]

When the goal of loving as God loves us seems impossible, John "does not suggest that we settle for something more manageable. He agrees that it is distant, and says that desire will get us there." Thus, as Matthew argues about John (and it is equally true of Teresa; indeed, this reality is critical to understanding the source of her profound humility and gratitude), "he never backs down from his statement of divine generosity."[44]

Teresa and John remind us of the power of love to motivate. They give us a lover's eagerness to love, to serve, to *be there* for the beloved, and to be a trustworthy presence for love to grow in our world. They help us to rise to the occasion of a love that holds us accountable to our own capacity for goodness and that asks us to incorporate all of our gifts and talents into a daily practice of generous self-offering. Additionally, they remind us that we cannot give what we do not have ... that we ourselves are often too myopic to see God's loving intention, for us and for our world. In fact, even when we know better, we can find ourselves easily discouraged, often depleted, and all the more needy of the constancy of God's loving energy, empowering us with the vision, insight, strength, and purpose that we and the world we inhabit *require*.

If human beings are our only teachers as to the nature and quality of love in action, and we do not go directly to the Source and Loving Teacher of all love for answers, insights, and lessons in the "how" and not just the "what" of love, we run the risk of blindly leading (or

43. Matthew, *Impact of God*, 33.
44. Ibid.

following) the blind. In fact, leaving sin and malice out of the equation altogether, the painful truth of the matter is that the frustrations of daily life, our own personal foibles, and the practical reality of being human often keep us from feeling and expressing the love that we might be capable of. What Teresa and John teach us, so beautifully, is that to love is to be in a constant process of purification and refinement. Always, always, we can learn to love more and better. This reality is not meant to dishearten us—although it could, easily, if we did not have a sound method of proceeding. This "method of proceeding" is precisely what Teresa and John set out to offer.

The "method" that they describe is prayer—what we might more typically call "contemplative prayer" that takes place in silence, stillness, and the interior of the human person. What they encourage us to consider is that there is "a world" within us—an absorbing world that is (at least, when it is attuned to the Spirit of God), far more real and reliable than the world we live in. They give us criteria for assessing the quality of our lives, and, even more importantly, for discerning the depth and reality of our lives. They understand that we live in a world that is swarming with multiple sources of authority, but with very little that is true, lasting, trustworthy, or meaningful. They demonstrate, convincingly, that authentic, life-giving love is the only foundation strong enough to provide the support we need, and they show us that even this foundation will shift like sand, until we anchor it completely and thoroughly in our love-relationship with God. They teach us the garden space of the heart—its fertility and its malleability as grace rains down like water, permeating the soil of our souls and piercing our being with shafts of light. They teach us that our days, which so often fill themselves with whatever comes, can instead be punctuated by the very breath of God, drawing us into fullness of life in a space of tenderness that whispers the truths by which we aspire to live.

2

Excerpts from Teresa's *Interior Castle*

First Dwelling Places

Prefatory Comment to Teresa:

Teresa of Avila's *Interior Castle* chronicles the progression of the soul's relationship with God through seven stages of increasing intimacy and depth. The seven *moradas*, or "dwelling places," convey where we are, developmentally, in terms of both our self-awareness and our relationship with God.

The First Dwelling Places represent a space of spiritual awakening as we become aware of our deeper reality as persons created in the image and likeness of God. Two scriptural references and three interconnected metaphors ground and convey this stage in the life of the human person. The first scriptural reference is to Gen. 1:26–27—the reminder that humanity was (and therefore, each of us is) "created in the image and likeness of God." Teresa uses this passage not as a point of reference to a past moment, but as a reflection on our origins that has no point of reference to history. To say that we are "created in the image and likeness of God" is to point to a timeless reality that each of us must discover for ourselves in order to determine its truth. The premise that the image of God resides within us then provides a grounding for entering ourselves in order to uncover, recover, and form a relationship with the God and the self who are embedded in the mystery of that process. The second scriptural reference is to John 14:2: "In God's house there are many rooms." If God is present in all of creation, this presence is a constant relational reality in which we are called to live intentionally. To be aware of God's presence in us and in others provides the necessary perspective for us to explore our possibilities as human beings, created both for a relationship (with God and others) and toward a purpose that, alone, we may not be able to realize. This relational context enables us to experience and explore the space of our being in a totally new way. While John's reference to "God's house" is traditionally understood (even translated, at times) as "heaven," Teresa reminds us that heaven is not a geographical but a relational reality—a qualitative way of being that God's indwelling presence, actuated in us, gives to all time and space. We are created for this relational reality, our being strains toward it, and we are meant to live it out, here and now. Such a realization imbues our existence with far deeper significance, possibility, and even urgency, as we see our longing to belong as a soulful way of understanding ourselves and our world. Teresa's language about the soul's beauty, its "great dignity" and value accentuates the esteem in which we are held by the One who created us.

Originally, in the *Book of her Life*, Teresa had described the soul not so much as a "castle made of crystal," but a "garden where God takes delight."[1] And the soul's progress toward union with God had been depicted in terms of four ways of watering that garden, each one requiring less active work on the part of the soul, until, in the fourth

---

1. L 11:6: "The beginner should take into account that she is beginning to make a garden in which God will delight, but in very unfruitful soil that has many weeds. His Majesty will pull out the weeds and plant flowers instead. So let's consider that this has already been done when a soul is determined to advance in prayer and has already begun a practice of prayer, and so, with the help of God, we must try, like good gardeners, to take care to water these plants so that they will not die off but instead will blossom with flowers that emit a great fragrance, so that our Lord will take pleasure there and will come often to this garden to delight amidst its virtues."

stage, the soul took in rain directly from heaven. Although Teresa's experiences of prayer eventually surpassed the stages of prayer described in the *Life*, the framework of the garden, fragrant and delightful, as a space for union with God, is not entirely superseded by the metaphor of the castle with many rooms. In fact, Teresa retains the garden image even in the *Interior Castle* (I:1:1), drawing upon it to reinforce the idea that we are created for a union that delights both us and God, and, however difficult that it may be for us to imagine when we are enmeshed in sin, God truly takes delight in us.

Passages from Teresa's *First Dwelling Places*

Today, while beseeching our Lord to speak for me because I could not come up with anything to say nor did I know how to get started in carrying out this obedience, there came to my mind what I shall now speak about, which will provide us with a foundation. And it is this: that we consider our soul to be like a castle made entirely out of a diamond or very clear crystal, in which there are many rooms,[2] just as in heaven there are many dwelling places; since, if we consider it well, sisters, the soul of the just person is actually a paradise where God takes delight.[3] And what do you think it will be like, this place where a king so powerful, so wise, so pure, so full of all good things, takes delight? I cannot find anything comparable to the great beauty and profound potential of the soul. And really, our own understanding, no matter how keen, can hardly comprehend such a thing, just as we cannot comprehend God, even though God has told us we are created in God's own image and likeness.[4] (IC I:1:1)

It is no small pity and confusion that, through our fault, we do not understand ourselves nor do we know who we are! Would it not show great ignorance, my daughters, for a person not to know who his parents are or what country she comes from? How much more blindness do we show when we don't try to come to know ourselves!

---

2. Cf John 14:2.
3. Prov. 8:31.
4. Gen. 1:26.

We get taken up by our bodies and think that's all there is to us, even though we have heard people tell us that we have souls. Yet we seldom consider all the great riches contained in the soul or Who we contain within us, and so we make little effort to preserve our own deepest beauty. (IC I:1:2)

So let us consider that this castle has, as I have said, many dwelling places: some up high, others down below, others on the sides; and in the center and middle of all, it has the main dwelling place, which is where the most secret things pass between the soul and God. It is necessary for you to take into account this comparison; perhaps God will be served by it to give you to understand something of the favors God is pleased to grant our souls, and all the different types of them, in so far as I have been able to understand what is possible. Indeed, it would be impossible for anyone to understand them all, since there are many of them—much less someone as wretched as I am. Still, it will give you great consolation, when the Lord gives you to understand it, to know what is possible. . . . (IC I:1:3)

Turning to our beautiful and delightful castle, now we should consider how we are to enter it. Here I seem to say something silly, because, if this castle is the soul, it's clear that there is no reason to really enter, since it is within us. How stupid to tell someone to enter in a room he is already in. But you should understand that there are many ways of being inside: many souls are in the outskirts of the castle, which are where those that guard it are, and they don't even really care about entering inside, nor do they know what a precious place it is, nor who is inside, nor even the rooms that it contains. You will already have heard in some books on prayer that the soul should enter into itself; well, that is what I mean. (IC I:1:5)

Insofar as I can tell, the doorway to enter into this castle is prayer and consideration. I don't mean mental more than vocal; since prayer must always be with consideration. The person who pays no attention to whom she is speaking and what she is asking and who is the one asking whom, isn't really praying, however much the lips may move. Anyone who has the habit of speaking with the Majesty of God as though speaking to a slave, without taking care to see how he is speaking, but saying whatever comes to his head or what he has said at other times, I don't think is praying. Please God may no Christian pray this way. (IC I:1:7)[5]

Before going on I want to say that you should consider what it would be like to see this brilliantly shining and beautiful castle, this pearl from the Orient, this tree of life planted in the very living waters of life—that is, in God—when it falls into mortal sin. There is no darker darkness nor anything more obscure and black. . . . For the works of a soul in a state of grace are like clear streams flowing from a crystal-clear fountain. They are clear, because they proceed from this fount of life in which the soul is planted like a tree, and that is why they are most pleasing in the eyes of both God and humankind. . . . But in the case of a soul that separates itself from this fountain by its own fault and plants itself in another [place] where the water is black and foul smelling, everything that flows from it is equally wretched and dirty. (IC I:2:1-2)

Here we should consider that the fountain and that resplendent sun that is in the center of the soul does not lose its splendor or beauty; it is always within her, and nothing can take away that beauty. But, if a very dark cloth is placed over top of a crystal that is in the sun, it's clear that, even though the sun still shines within it, its clarity will not have the same effect on the crystal. (IC I:2:3)

We always hear about what a good thing prayer is . . . yet only what we ourselves can do in prayer is explained to us; little is explained about what the Lord works in a soul [through prayer]; I mean about the supernatural. (IC I:2:7)

Turning back to our castle with many dwelling places: you shouldn't think of these dwelling places as if they were in line, one after the other, but keep your eyes on the center, which is the room or palace where the king is, and consider a palmetto plant that has many coverings surrounding the flavorful part that you get to in the middle.

---

5. Teresa's basic, working definition of prayer, taken from L 8:5, is: "Prayer is nothing more than intimate conversation with a friend. It means taking time frequently to be alone with the One whom we know loves us."

It's the same way here: all around this central room there are many rooms. For the things of the soul must always be considered plentiful, spacious and large; it is difficult to exaggerate the abundance and generosity of the soul. It is capable of much more than we can imagine, and the light of God in this palace shines in all parts. And this is important for all people who pray, whether they pray a little or a great deal: one should never hold oneself back, nor stay in a corner. Instead, let yourself walk all around these dwelling places—up and down and all around, since God has given us such great dignity. Only then can we prepare ourselves to enter the place where God resides. (IC I:2:8)

Second Dwelling Places

Prefatory Comment to Teresa:

If we take Teresa's invitation to self-knowledge seriously and enter into the castle of the soul, we proceed rather rapidly to the second dwelling places, where we actually begin to hear the voice of our Beloved, God, calling us gently to approach the inner center of ourselves. The deepening awareness of the presence of God within us brings with it an increased responsibility to *become* a person ready, willing, and able to take on the high calling of authentic, adult relationship with God. As we "begin to realize that our understanding of ourselves has been partial at best and false at worst," we are placed in the midst of the dilemma of making difficult choices away from our more ordinary habits and patterns and toward cultivating that relationship.[6] Teresa refers to the soul at this stage as "mute"—that is, unable to respond appropriately to the loving call of God to partnership—and therefore, keenly aware of the need for grace. As I have noticed before:

> In the second dwelling places, the soul hears the call of God to a deeper, more godly way of life, and the soul desires to be good—to heed and respond to this call. But, as it realizes repeatedly that it is unable to do so, it can feel crushed with shame. This is a humbling kind of self-knowledge, at times painful to the soul, as it crashes against its own limitations. . . .

6. Ahlgren, *Entering*, 31–32.

> Here the soul learns its own radical need for grace, not as a foreign force, but as an orientation to goodness that works through and with us, awakened by the voice of God deep within.[7]

What is "humbling" is the awareness that, despite our knowledge, despite our good intentions, we often do not act in accordance with what is best, for ourselves and for others. This kind of self-knowledge builds in us a salvific kind of contrition that enables us to reach for the grace we need, as both a motivator and a habit.[8] Augustine puts this, most classically, as the dilemma of the divided will, which he describes so poignantly in *Confessions* book 8 and which Teresa tells us had a strong impact on her.[9] The First Week of Ignatius Loyola's *Spiritual Exercises*, which had formed and shaped Teresa, also calls us to hold the tension of our created potential and our fallen reality, in order to engage the will and choose toward a relationship with Christ.

If life in God consists in realizing one's true potential, and realizing one's true potential is not possible outside of a conscious and deliberate relationship with the One who knows us better than we know ourselves, the second dwelling places brings with it

> . . . the pain in discovering that we have made life choices that have brought us into conflict with our own potential as persons. Few people have the inherent or acquired self-knowledge at early stages of their lives to recognize their own deepest potential; but the experience of the second dwelling places increasingly calls us into a greater knowledge of who we were meant to be and a greater desire to become that person.[10]

Passages from Teresa's Second Dwelling Places

Now let us speak about souls that enter the second dwelling places and what they do in them. . . . This stage pertains to those who have already begun to practice prayer and have understood how important it is not to stay in the first dwelling places. But they still don't have

---

7. Ibid., 32–33.
8. See Aquinas, *Summa theologiae* q. 113.
9. See *Confessions* books 7 and 8, especially 8:23–24. Teresa describes the impact on her of reading Augustine's *Confessions* in L 9:7–8, and she even cites *Confessions* 10:20 in L 13:3. She would have read the *Confessions* shortly after it appeared in Spanish in 1554.
10. *Entering*, 35.

the determination to remain in this second stage without turning back, for they don't avoid the occasions of sin, which is very dangerous. May they at least try to spend some time avoiding the snakes and poisonous things that have entered with them, for this is a great blessing. (IC II:1:1–2)

People in these rooms, in some sense, have much more work than in the first, although there is not as much danger, and there is great hope that they will enter further into the castle. I say that they have to work harder here, because those who are in the first dwelling places are like deaf-mutes and thus they bear more easily the trial of not being able to speak. But this trial is much harder on those who can hear but cannot speak. Still that does not mean that they would not want to hear, since it is always a great thing to understand what is said to us. So these people in the second dwelling places can hear God's callings, since they are getting closer to where His Majesty resides. God is a good neighbor, and God's goodness and loving kindness is such that, even when we are caught up in pastimes and business affairs and pleasures and trivial things and even falling into sin and rising again (because these creatures are so poisonous and always agitating and their company is so dangerous that it is a wonder that we don't get tripped up by them and fall), still Our Lord desires greatly that we love Him and seek out His company. And thus God never stops inviting us to draw closer. And this whisper of love is so sweet that the poor soul dissolves at not doing immediately what is asked. This is why I say that it is far harder than not hearing anything. (IC II:1:2)

I am not saying that these whispers and callings are like others that I will describe later. Rather, they come to us through words spoken by other good people, or through sermons, or through what is read in good books, or through illnesses and trials, or sometimes through a truth that we glimpse during the moments when we are in prayer. (And even if those moments in prayer are brief and rather tepid, God esteems them a great deal.) And you, my sisters, should not underestimate this initial favor, nor become disheartened if you do not respond immediately to God. For God knows well how to wait patiently many days and even years, especially when God sees perseverance and good intentions. That perseverance is what is most necessary here, for, with perseverance, one can eventually overcome nearly anything. But the battery of assaults made by the devil here are ferocious. The soul encounters a thousand obstacles and feels more keenly these trials than it did in the first dwelling places, because there the soul was deaf and dumb, and it heard very little and resisted even less, as one who has no hope of overcoming the resistance. But here, the understanding is more alive and the faculties more capable, and the soul cannot help but hear all of the blows of the artillery striking it. For here the adversaries manifest through these snakes all kinds of worldly things, making us think that they are everlasting: the esteem one has in the world, our friends and family, one's health (especially as one dedicates oneself to penance, which souls entering into this dwelling place always want to start practicing in some form), and thousands more impediments. (IC II:1:3)

Oh, Jesus! What an uproar the devils instigate here. And the afflictions of the poor soul, who now does not know whether to plow forward or turn back to the first room. . . . The will is inclined to love, because it has already seen such countless tokens and signs of love, and it would want to repay some of them. What especially becomes apparent and the soul can never forget is how this true Lover never leaves her, accompanying her and giving her life and being. And then the intellect helps it to understand that it could not possibly have a better friend, even if it lived for many years, and that the world is full of much falsity, and that all of the distractions that the devil places before it are full of trials, worries, and contradictions. Then it tells the soul to be certain that outside of this castle it will find neither security nor peace. It should avoid going about to strange houses since its own is so filled with blessings to be enjoyed if it wants. Indeed, it asks: Who else already has everything they need in their own home, and, especially, who has such a guest within who will make her the owner of all good things, provided that she keeps from getting lost, like the prodigal son who ended up eating the food of swine?[11] (IC II:1:4)

Oh, good Lord! Your help is so necessary here! Without it we cannot do anything. In Your mercy, do not let this soul be deceived and then leave off what she has begun! Give her light so that she can see how all of her well-being is contained here, so that she turns away from bad companions. What a wonderful thing it is to speak with others who have experience in this castle, and to approach not only those whom she sees are already in the same room she is in, but also to speak with those whom she understands have entered the rooms closer to the center. Talking with them will be a great help to her, for they will draw her to the places where they are. And may she always be careful not to let herself be overcome. If the devil sees her with a strong commitment to lose her life and the rest and all that he offers before she would ever turn back to the first dwelling places, he will leave her alone all the faster. May she be strong[12] and not like those who knelt down to drink before going into battle (I don't remember whom);[13] but rather may she commit herself to fight against these devils and to realize that there are no better weapons than those of the cross. (IC II:1:6)

Although I have said this at other times, it is so important that I am going to repeat it again here: that is that to remember that there are no real consolations in this beginning stage. That would be a poor way of starting to build up such a precious and great castle. If we begin on sand, everything will fall to the ground; and you will not be able to move forward through challenges and temptations. These are not the dwelling places where manna rains from heaven. They are farther on, where everything tastes sweet because the soul in those places wants only want God wants. What an amusing thing that even though we still have a thousand obstructions and imperfections ahead, and our

---

11. Cf. Luke 15:16.
12. Literally, "be a man," *varón.*
13. cf. Judg. 7:5. This is the story of God helping Gideon to sort out the best soldiers before the battle of Midian. Those who knelt down to drink were considered the weaker of the two groups. John of the Cross uses this very same analogy in a letter he wrote of uncertain date to a Carmelite nun in Madrid, perhaps in 1586: "Daughter, in the emptiness and dryness of all things, God tries us to see who are the strong soldiers who will win the battle. They are the ones who know how to drink water in the air without sinking down to the ground, just as the soldiers of Gideon, who won with empty jars of dried mud and candles lit inside them, which are symbols of the dryness of the senses and the good and enkindled spirit within." See John of the Cross, Letter 5 in *CWJC,* 687.

virtues have not grown to the point that we can move forward (since they are just being born in us—and please God that they are being born!), yet we have no shame about wanting to take delight in prayer and we complain about dryness. May you never be like this, sisters; embrace the cross that your Spouse carried, and understand that this must be your work. May the one who can endure more commit herself to enduring more for God's sake, and she will be the most freed; and if God grants you other favors, as a by-product, give great thanks. (IC II:1:7)

The whole aim of any person who is beginning prayer—and don't forget this because it's very important—should be to work and commit and prepare herself to bring her will into conformity with the will of God. Be certain that, as I shall say later, the greatest perfection attainable along the spiritual path lies in this conformity. Whoever lives in more perfect conformity with God's will, will receive more from God and will move farther along on this journey. . . . Let us try to do what is in us to do—which is to protect ourselves from these poisonous vermin, for the Lord often desires that dryness and bad thoughts afflict and pursue us without our being able to get rid of them. Sometimes God even permits these reptiles to bite us so that afterward we may know how to guard ourselves better and can prove whether we are greatly grieved by our sins. (IC II:1:8)

Thus, if you should at times fall, don't become discouraged and stop striving to advance. For even from this fall God will draw out good, as does the seller of an antidote who drinks some poison in order to test whether his antidote is effective. Even if the only way we saw our misery and the great harm that it does us to run about wasting ourselves was through the massive struggle we have in turning inward and recollecting ourselves, that would be enough. Can there be an evil greater than that of being ill at ease in our own house? What hope can we have of finding rest outside of ourselves if we cannot be at rest within? . . . Believe me, if we don't obtain and have peace in our own house we will not find it outside. (IC II:1:9)

Such disturbances are set up here by the devil. Remember that you cannot begin to recollect yourselves by force but only by gentleness, if your recollection is going to be more continual. (IC II:1:10)

I have already told you that the door of entry to this castle is prayer. Well now, it is foolish to think that we will enter heaven without entering into ourselves, coming to know ourselves, reflecting on our misery and what we owe God, and asking God often for mercy. (IC II:1:11)

Third Dwelling Places

Prefatory Comment to Teresa:

In the third dwelling places, the soul experiences a growing fortitude that is rooted in its first major accomplishment: the union of wills. The moral struggles of the earlier dwelling places are resolved, as the individual acquires the habit of virtue and is less inclined toward anything that compromises her or his integrity. Entry into this stage "symbolizes something of a moral victory for the soul, as its dedication to prayer has led it to a state in which it is less inclined to thoughtless behavior and what Teresa calls 'occasions of sin.'"[14] We could understand the third dwelling places, then, as a space of greater mindfulness, intentionality and personal integration, characterized by greater moral integrity and a growing consistency and predictability as a human being. People in this state are trustworthy and enjoy being good.

However, because they are prompt to do the right thing and live their lives by the commandments, people in the third dwelling places may presume God's favor or think of relationship with God as a sort of transaction: "If I abide by God's law, I will get rewarded." This stage "represents either a point of entry into deeper, transformative relationship with God or the end of the road for those who equate religion with its codes, creeds, and rituals."[15] Teresa uses the example of the rich young man from the gospel who chose to "walk away sad"

---

14. Ahlgren, *Entering*, 39.
15. Ibid.

rather than heed the call to "come, follow me." She warns people here not to feel entitled to a reward for doing what they ought to do, but rather, to enter into true relationship with God which, by definition, will change everything.[16]

In John's mystical corpus, this stage parallels what is covered in *The Ascent of Mount Carmel*, especially where John speaks of "desiring, for the sake of Christ, to enter into poverty, emptiness and self-stripping with respect to all that there is in the world,"[17] so that, "free of all that is dissimilar to or not in conformity with God," the person can "come to receive the likeness of God."[18] As they both suggest, somehow we tend to prefer our own likeness to that of God.

Passages from Teresa's Third Dwelling Places

What shall we say to those who through perseverance and by the mercy of God have won these battles and have entered the third dwelling places, if not: "blessed is the one who fears the Lord?"[19] Certainly, we are right in calling such people blessed, since if they do not turn back, they are, from what we can understand, on the secure path toward their salvation. And so you see, sisters, how important it is to win these past battles, for I am certain the Lord never fails to give persons like this security of conscience, which is no small blessing. I said "security" and I was wrong, for there is no security in this life; so always understand that I mean "if they don't abandon the path they began on." (IC III:1:1)

Through the goodness of God, I believe that there are many of these souls in the world. They strongly desire not to offend God, even guarding themselves against minor sins. They do penance, and they set aside time for prayer and recollection. They are careful to spend their

---

16. See Pedro Arrupe: "Nothing is more practical than finding God—that is, than falling in Love in a quite absolute, final way. What you are in love with, what seizes your imagination, will affect everything. It will decide what will get you out of bed in the morning, what you do with your evenings, how you spend your weekends, what you read, whom you know, what breaks your heart, and what amazes you with joy and gratitude. Fall in Love, stay in love, and it will decide everything."
17. AMC I:13, p. 82 below.
18. AMC II:5:4, see p. 83 below.
19. Ps. 111:1.

time well, and they practice charity toward their neighbors. They are very balanced in their use of speech and dress and how they govern their houses, those who have them. Certainly, this is a state to be desired, and it seems that there is no reason to deny them entrance all the way to the last dwelling place—nor will the Lord deny it to them, if they want it, for this desire is an excellent way to prepare themselves so that God will grant them this favor. (III:1:5)

Oh, Jesus! And who will say that they do not want such a great good, especially after having passed through the previous trials? No, no one will. We all say that we want it. But there is need of still more, in order that the soul possess the Lord completely. It is not enough to say we want it, just as this was not enough for the rich young man when the Lord told him what one must do in order to be perfect.[20] From the time I began to speak of these dwelling places I have had this young man in mind, because we are just like him, and ordinarily our great dryness in prayer comes from this, although it also has other causes . . . But [like him] these souls cannot bear with patience that the door to the place where our king stays is closed to them, when they consider themselves his faithful servants, which they are. But the king has many servants here on earth, and not all of them enter his chamber. Enter, enter, my daughters, into your interior; move forward with your little works, for, as Christians, you owe all of this and much more, and it is enough that you are faithful servants of God. Do not wish for too much and then find yourselves with nothing. Look at the saints who entered the chamber of this king, and you will see the difference between them and us. Do not ask for what you have not yet merited, nor should it even enter our minds that we should merit this, for however much we may serve, we who have offended God. (III:1:6)

Oh humility, humility! . . . I cannot believe that whoever makes such a big deal out of these drynesses is lacking somewhat in humility. . . . Let us prove ourselves, my sisters, or may God try us, as well God knows how to do, even if we often do not want to understand that we are being tested. Let us look at these souls who are so well ordered and

20. See Matt. 19:16–22.

let us see what they do for God and then we will see how we have no reason to complain about God, since, if we turn our backs and go away sad, like the young man in the gospel,[21] when God tells us what we must do to be perfect, what do you want His Majesty to do? For God must reward us in conformity with the love we have for God. And this love, daughters, must not be fabricated in our imaginations, but proven by our actions. And don't think that God really needs our works; rather, God needs the determination of our wills. (IC III:1:7)

I have known some souls—and I believe I can even say many souls—who have reached this state and have lived many years in this righteous and well-ordered way, both in body and soul. . . . But then, when God tries them in some minor matters, they get so disturbed and sick at heart that it bewilders and even frightens me. It is useless to try to give them advice, since, because they have been virtuous for so long, they think they can teach everyone else and that there is nothing left for them to learn. (IC III:2:1)

I have found no way of consoling such people, if not to show great sympathy for their pain—and, truth be told, they do seem rather pathetic—and not to contradict their reasoning. For everything in their minds leads them to believe that they suffer these things for God, and they can't even see that this is an imperfection on their part; it is another mistake that advanced people can fall into. And we should not be surprised at what they experience, although I do think that they should be able to get over their feelings about such things. For there are many occasions when God wants God's chosen ones to experience their misery and so God withdraws God's favor somewhat. And little more than that is necessary, since we clearly know ourselves well immediately. And they understand right away this way of being tested, because they understand their faults clearly, and sometimes they feel badly at seeing how easily and without being able to help themselves they get bogged down with trivial things. I hold this to be a great kindness of God, and, although it is a defect, it becomes very beneficial for humility. (IC III:2:2)

21. See Matt. 19:22.

But these people I am talking about do not do this. Rather, they canonize their feelings in their minds and would like others to do so. I shall give some examples, so that we understand and test ourselves first, before God tests us, since it would be better to be prepared and to have understood ourselves beforehand. (IC III:2:3)

A rich person, without children and without anyone whom he might want to favor as an heir, loses his wealth—but not to an extent that he lacks what is necessary for himself and for the good of his household; in fact he has more than he needs. If this person goes around greatly disturbed and as anxious as if he hadn't even bread to eat, how is our Lord going to ask him to leave all for God? Then the person gives the excuse that he wants greater comfort so that he can give to the poor. But I believe that God prefers that we conform ourselves to what His Majesty wants, and that we keep our souls at rest, rather than observing that kind of charity. And if this person is unable to act with equanimity because God has not brought him that far, well and good; but he should at least understand that he greatly lacks freedom of spirit. And thus he should prepare himself so that God might give it to him, because he certainly will be asked for it. (IC III:2:4)

Or a person has plenty to eat and even a surplus. And then it turns out that he can acquire more wealth. Well, all right: let him take the wealth if it is given to him. But when that happens and he possesses it but then strives for more and more, no matter how good his intention may be (and these are virtuous, prayerful people, as I have said, so he should have this); still he need have no fear of ascending any farther to the dwelling places closest to the king. (IC III:2:4)

There is a similar occurrence when an opportunity presents itself for such persons to be despised or lose a little of their honor. Even if God grants them this favor of enduring such a thing (for God is very fond of favoring virtue publicly so that virtue itself will not undergo a loss of esteem; or perhaps God does this because they have been good servants, for this Beloved of ours is very good), still they are left so disturbed in spirit that they cannot help themselves, nor can they get over such a thing very quickly. God help me! Aren't these the same ones who for a long while now have been considering how the Lord suffered and how good it is to endure and they even desire such a thing? But then they want everything to be just as ordered as they carry out their lives, and please God that they may not think that what they are suffering is someone else's fault and then think themselves meritorious because of it. (IC III:2:5)

It must seem to you, sisters, that I am getting off track and am not really addressing you, because such things do not happen to us here, since we neither have an income, nor do we desire or strive for it, nor does anyone do us injury. For this reason, these examples are not what happens to us, but from them, we can see other things that can happen. And we need not describe them. But in this way you will see whether or not you are truly stripped of all that you have left behind. Because little things happen, perhaps not of this sort, but in which you can very easily see whether or not you are in charge of your own passions. And believe me, this is not about whether or not we wear a religious habit; it is about whether or not we are growing in virtue and we seek to surrender our will to that of God in everything and if the whole of our lives are ordered in the way God ordains and in desiring that God's will, not ours, be done. Until we arrive at that point, as I have said: humility, the ointment for all of our wounds. If there is true humility, even if we must wait for a while, the physician, who is God, will come to heal us. (IC III:2:6)

Love has not yet reached the point of overwhelming reason. But I should like us to use our reason to make ourselves dissatisfied with this [well-ordered] way of serving God, always going step by step, for we'll never finish this journey. And since, in our opinion, we are continually walking and are tired (for, believe me, it is a wearisome journey), we will be doing quite well if we don't go astray. But does it seem to you, daughters, that if we could go from one land to another in eight days, it would be good to take a year through wind, snow, rain, and bad roads? Wouldn't it be better to make the journey all at once? For all of these obstacles present themselves—as well as the danger of serpents. Oh, what good proofs I could give of these things. And please God that I may have passed beyond this stage, for often enough it seems to me that I have not. (IC III:2:7)

Since we are so circumspect, everything offends us because we fear everything; so we don't dare go further—as if we could reach these dwelling places while leaving to other persons the trouble of treading the path for us. Since this is not possible, let us exert ourselves, my sisters, for the love of God, to abandon our reason and our fears into God's hands. . . . We should care only about moving quickly so as to see this Lord.[22] (IC III:2:8)

With humility present, this stage is a most excellent one. If humility is lacking, we will remain here our whole lives—and with a thousand afflictions and miseries. For when we have not abandoned ourselves, this state is very laborious and burdensome. We shall be walking while weighted down with this mud of our human misery, which is not so with those who ascend to the remaining rooms. And in those rooms further on Our Lord never fails to pay us well, and even generously. For the consolations God gives are far greater than those we find in the comforts and distractions of life. (IC III:2:9) And they come to us brimming over with love and fortitude by which we can journey with less labor and grow in the practice of works and virtue. (IC III:2:11)

To make progress here we must seek out someone who is very free from illusion about the things of the world. For in order to know ourselves, it helps a great deal to speak with someone who already knows the world for what it is. It also helps because when we see others doing things that seem impossible, it encourages us to be bold in imitation. (IC III:2:12)

Fourth Dwelling Places

Prefatory Comment to Teresa:

These beautiful passages describe the graced process of "enlarging the heart"—the quickening and swelling of the human heart, facilitated by

---

22. Implicit here is the image of the bride of the Song of Songs and her pressured movement through the streets seeking her beloved; cf. Song of Songs 3:2, 5:6b.

God. This is both a scriptural concept and one that is often discussed in the history of spirituality, deeply related to the tradition's concept of "purity of heart." Scripturally, Teresa derives it from Ps. 118:32 and speaks of the expansion of the heart, or the development of the soul's capacity to love in God-given ways that "swell the heart and produce ineffable blessings."[23] As Teresa teaches here, this process is absolutely essential to spiritual progress; no further growth is possible unless the soul develop within itself the capacity to love. She also articulates in this section her basic spiritual principle, one that grounds all spiritual and personal discernment: we are to do what "best stirs us to love."[24]

Another basic spiritual practice comes to the fore in this stage: we come to realize that, no matter what our personal circumstances, we can always bring a loving disposition to bear in every moment. This realization becomes a critical way of connecting with God and beginning to develop a relational habit of turning to God, of bringing relationship with God into everything that we do. In identifying its capacity to love God in all circumstances and to draw strength from that relationship, the soul is empowered with deeper, previously unknown capacities within itself: patience, new vision, new possibilities. Even our own inconstancy, our tendency to distraction, and our restlessness can be tolerated without losing inner peace and connection with God around and through such distraction. She writes: "Perhaps we do not know what love is . . . it doesn't consist in great delight but in desiring with strong determination to please God in everything . . ."[25]

In this section, Teresa generously reveals her own struggles with prayer and wants us to understand that prayer does not consist, necessarily, of always thinking about God. Prayer is more about opening oneself to God's presence as one is, where one is, wherever that is. There is no one correct way to pray. But we do always have

---

23. IC IV:2:6.
24. IC IV:1:7: "I only wish to inform you that in order to profit by this path and ascend to the dwelling places we desire, the important thing is not to think much, but to love much; and so do that which best stirs love in you."
25. IC IV:1:7.

the capacity to cultivate a loving disposition. The signs of love are our desire to reach out in compassion; as long as we do that, we are *already* praying. Teresa's advice about prayer is deeply practical. She admits that it is difficult to "erase" our minds when we sit in contemplative prayer when she writes, "Ordinarily the mind flies about quickly; only God can hold it fast in such a way as to make it seem that we are somehow loosed from this body."[26] In fact, Teresa admits, "I have been very afflicted at times in the midst of this turmoil of mind. . . . It was an arduous thing for me that [my intellect] should be so restless at times."[27] Her pastoral advice here reveals the same kind of tolerant tenderness that people appreciated in John of the Cross.[28] And she urges us to be gently tolerant of our own inadequacies when we try to settle into quiet:

> Any disquiet and war can be suffered if we find peace where we live, as I have already said. But that we want to rest from the thousand trials there are in the world and that God wants to prepare us for rest and that within ourselves lies the disturbance cannot be anything but painful and even unbearable. These miseries will not afflict or assail everyone as much as they did me for many years because I was so wretched. But since it was something so painful for me, I think perhaps that it will be for you, too. And so I say that it is an unavoidable thing and should not be a disturbance or affliction for you. We must let the millclapper keep clacking on, and must continue grinding our flour, not stopping our work with the will and the understanding.[29]

Passages from Teresa's Fourth Dwelling Places:

In order to begin to speak of the fourth dwelling places I really need to entrust myself, as I've already done, to the Holy Spirit, to speak for me from here on, so that I may say something about the remaining rooms in a way that you will understand. For supernatural experiences begin here. And it is very difficult to explain them, if God does not do so, as happened in another place in which was written what I could, up

26. IC IV:1:8.
27. Ibid.
28. See DN I:10:1–2, below, pp. 89–90.
29. IC IV:1:12–13.

to then, understand, some fourteen years ago, more or less. And even though I believe I am a little more enlightened now about these favors that God bestows on some souls, it is another thing completely to know how to explain them. (IC IV:1:1)

Since these dwelling places now are closer to where God is, their beauty is great. There are things to see and understand so delicate that the intellect is incapable of devising a way to explain them. Something might come out that seems right and not too obscure for those who lack experience, and those who have experience will understand very well, especially if they have a lot of experience. (IC IV:1:2)

Poisonous things rarely enter in these dwelling places, and, if they do enter, they do no real harm, but rather they often leave behind some benefit. (IC IV:1:3)

In speaking about what I said would explain concerning the difference between consolations and spiritual delights, the term 'consolations,' I think, can be given to those experiences we ourselves acquire through our own meditation and petitions to the Lord, those that proceed from our own nature. Of course, God helps in them, for it must be understood in all that I say that we can do nothing without God. But these arise from the virtuous work that we do, and it seems that we have earned them through our effort, and with some reason it gives us some consolation to have employed ourselves in such work. And, if we consider this, we can even have some of the same consolation in many things that can happen to us on earth—as when someone suddenly inherits a great fortune, or when we suddenly see a person that we love very much. . . . It seems to me that, just as these consolations are natural, so are those that are given to us by God (although those are of a more noble origin, even though the other type are not bad). In sum, they begin in our own [human] nature and end in God. The spiritual delights, on the other hand, begin in God, but our human nature feels them and delights in them as much as the others that I mentioned—and much more. O Jesus, how I long to know how to explain this! Because I understand that there is a great difference between the two, and yet do not have the knowledge to explain it; may the Lord do it for me! (IC IV:1:4)

Now I remember a line we say in prayer, "When you have expanded my heart."[30] To those with a lot of experience, this will be enough to see the difference there is between one and the other, and those who don't have experience will need more. The spiritual consolations that I spoke of do not swell the heart.[31] (IC IV:1:5)

In order to truly profit by this path and ascend to the dwelling places we desire, the important thing is not to think much, but to love much; and so do that which best stirs love in you. Perhaps we do not know what loving is; that would not surprise me. For love does not consist in great delight but in desiring with the greatest determination to please God in everything and to try as best we can not to offend God and to pray for the advancement of the honor and glory of Christ and the increase of the Catholic Church. These are the signs of love. And do not think that everything comes down to thinking of nothing but that and that if you become a little distracted all is lost. (IC IV:1:7)

Oh, Lord: take into account all that we suffer on this path because of our lack of understanding! The trouble is that because we think that there is nothing more to do than think of You, we do not even know how to ask those who know, nor do we understand what there is to ask. And thus we suffer terrible trials because we do not understand ourselves.[32] And what is not really bad but good we think is a great fault. This lack of knowledge causes the afflictions of many people who engage in prayer and their complaints about interior trials—at least in people without much education, and then they become saddened

---

30. Ps. 118:32.
31. The theme of the expansion of the heart is contained in a number of treatises; Teresa would have been familiar with Augustine's development of this prayer in Book 1 of the Confessions: "Narrow is the mansion of my soul; enlarge Thou it, that Thou mayest enter in. It is ruinous; repair Thou it. It has that within which must offend Thine eyes; I confess and know it. But who shall cleanse it? or to whom should I cry, save Thee? Lord, cleanse me from my secret faults, and spare Thy servant from the power of the enemy. I believe, and therefore do I speak. Lord, Thou knowest. Have I not confessed against myself my transgressions unto Thee, and Thou, my God, hast forgiven the iniquity of my heart? I contend not in judgment with Thee, who art the truth; I fear to deceive myself; lest mine iniquity lie unto itself. Therefore I contend not in judgment with Thee; for if Thou, Lord, shouldest mark iniquities, O Lord, who shall abide it?"
32. Again, cf. DN 1:10:1–4.

and lose their health and even give up altogether. These people do not consider that there is an interior world here within us. And just as we cannot stop the movement of the heavens, but rather it proceeds in rapid motion, neither can we stop the movement of our own thoughts, and then the faculties of the soul go with it, and we think that we are lost and have wasted the time we have spent before God. But the soul is perhaps completely joined with God in the dwelling places that are very close, while the mind is on the outskirts of the castle suffering from a thousand wild and poisonous beasts, and meriting by this suffering. As a result, we should not be disturbed, nor should we abandon prayer, for that is what the devil would want us to do. And for the most part all of these trials and disturbances come from our not knowing ourselves. (IC IV:1:9)

Any disquiet and war can be suffered if we find peace where we live, as I have already said. But that we want to rest from the thousand trials there are in the world and that God wants to prepare us for this rest, and that within ourselves lies the disturbance cannot be anything but painful and even unbearable. (IC IV:1:12)

These miseries will not afflict or assail everyone as much as they did me for many years because I was so wretched. It seems almost that I myself wanted to take vengeance on myself. And since this was so painful for me, I think that perhaps it will be for you, too. And so I often speak of it here and there, so that I might arrive at explaining to you that it is an unavoidable thing and should not be a disturbance or affliction for you. We must let the millclapper keep clacking on, and must continue grinding our flour, not stopping our work with the will and the understanding.[33] (IC IV:1:13)

It seems that I have explained about spiritual consolations. . . . (IC IV:2:1) What I call the spiritual delights, which in another place I called the prayer of quiet,[34] are very different, and anyone who has, by the kindness of God, experienced them will know this right away. Let's

33. Compare with her description of her own experience of prayer in L 17:5–7.
34. See L chapters 14–15.

consider, in order to understand this better, that we see two fountains with two water troughs that fill with water.... (IC IV:2:2)

Now these two troughs are filled with water in different ways; with one the water comes from far away through many aqueducts and devices; with the other the source of the water is right there, and the trough fills without any noise. If the spring is abundant, as is this one we are speaking about, the water overflows once the trough is filled, forming a large stream. There is no need of any other device, nor the help of aqueducts, because the water is always flowing from the spring. (IC IV:2:3)

And the difference between the one that comes by way of aqueducts is the consolations that I have spoken of, which are derived from meditation and thus they come from our thoughts, using creatures to help our meditation and tiring the intellect. And since they come, after all, from our own efforts, they make noise when there has to be some replenishing of the benefits the consolation causes in the soul. (IC IV:2:3)

With this other fountain, the water comes from its own source, which is God . . . [who] produces this delight with the greatest peace and quiet and sweetness in the very interior part of ourselves. I do not know from where or how, for one does not feel the joy and delight in the heart, the way one would with earthly consolations, especially at the beginning. But afterward it [the delight] fills everything; this water overflows through all the dwelling places and faculties until reaching the body. That is why I said that it begins in God and ends in ourselves. For certainly, as anyone who has experienced this will know, the entire exterior person also enjoys its savor and sweetness. (IC IV:2:4)

I was now considering, as I was writing this, that in the verse that I mentioned, "When you have expanded my heart," it says that the heart expanded. But I don't think the experience is something, as I say, that rises from the heart, but from another part still more interior, as from something deep. I think this must be the center of the soul.... (IC IV:2:5)

Turning to the verse and how it might help me to explain something, what I think is helpful is the idea of expansion. It seems that since heavenly water begins to rise from this spring I'm mentioning that is deep within us, it swells and expands our whole interior being, producing ineffable blessings. The soul does not even understand what is given it here. . . . This spiritual delight is not something that can be imagined because however diligent our efforts we cannot acquire it. The very experience of it makes us realize that it is not of the same metal as we ourselves but fashioned from the purest gold of the divine wisdom. Here, in my opinion, the faculties are not united by absorbed and looking, as though in wonder, at what they see. (IC IV:2:6)

You will ask me how then one can obtain these spiritual delights without seeking them. . . . The initial thing necessary for such favors is to love God without self-interest. (IC IV:2:9)

When God wants to grant us this favor, one noticeably senses a gentle drawing inward . . . like a hedgehog curling up or a turtle drawing into its shell. . . . So the soul instead of striving to engage in discourse strives to remain attentive and aware of what the Lord is working in it. (IC IV:3:3–4)

These interior works are all gentle and peaceful. . . . Leave the soul here in God's hands; let God do what God will with it, with the greatest disinterest about your own benefit possible and the greatest turning over of the self into God. (IC IV:3:6)

And without any effort or noise let the soul try to cut down the flow of the intellect, but do not suspend it, nor the mind either. For it is good to remember that it is in God's presence and who this God is. If all of this absorbs it, that is fine. But let it not try to understand what is happening to it, because this is given to the will. Let the soul enjoy God's presence without any endeavors other than some loving words . . . and often the intellect will be suspended, even though only for a short time. (IC IV:3:7)

What an expansion or dilation of the soul is may be clearly understood from the example of a fount whose water doesn't overflow into a stream because the fountain itself is constructed of such material that the more water there is flowing into it the larger the trough becomes. So it seems is the case with this prayer and with many other marvels that God grants to the soul, for God is enabling and preparing it so that it can keep everything within itself. Hence this interior sweetness and expansion can be verified in the fact that the soul is not as tied down as it was before in things pertaining to the service of God, but has much more freedom . . . and is left with a great confidence that it will, indeed, enjoy God. (IC IV:3:9)

Fifth Dwelling Places

Prefatory Comment to Teresa:

It is in the fifth dwelling places that we begin to understand the particularity and depth of God's love for us. God becomes known in a more profound and intimate way, as here the soul "comes to understand that God cherishes it particularly and has chosen it for union, in the same deliberate way that spouses choose and dedicate themselves to each other."[35] With the "expansion of the heart" that has been accomplished in the fourth dwelling places, the journey toward union with God has taken a critical turn. Now, it is time to understand ourselves in the light of the love of God, which gives each one of us a unique identity as "chosen." Teresa herself frames this stage in the journey around the text in Matthew's gospel: "Many are called but few are chosen."[36]

"Chosenness" sets us apart by emphasizing our uniqueness and inviting us into the miracle expressed in and through our being created. If we are created in God's own image and carved out of God's hand, we are also, each of us, invited to express God's Godness in the particular way that God takes flesh in us and in our lives. As she encourages us to know ourselves in light of the empowering relationship with God that is growing and being grown in us, Teresa reminds us that all we must do is dig deeply within to "find the hidden treasure which truly lies within us."[37]

35. Ahlgren, *Entering*, 63. See discussion, 63–75.
36. Matt. 20:16; see IC V:1:2.

In the fifth dwelling places, the soul comes to know her "chosen-ness"—that is, her identity as God's cherished one. In his *Life of the Beloved*, Henri Nouwen elucidates this concept by writing:

> It is very hard for me to express well the depth of meaning the word "chosen" has for me, but I hope you are willing to listen to me from within. From all eternity, long before you were born and became a part of history, you existed in God's heart. Long before your parents admired you or your friends acknowledged your gifts or your teachers, colleagues, and employers encouraged you, you were already "chosen." The eyes of love had seen you as precious, as of infinite beauty, as of eternal value. When love chooses, it chooses with a perfect sensitivity for the unique beauty of the chosen one, and it chooses without making anyone feel excluded.[38]

The realms of the fifth dwelling places encompass longer unitive encounters with God, qualitatively different from forms of union that the soul has experienced previously. They are absorbing, and the person's normal cognitive abilities are temporarily diminished. Teresa speaks of these encounters as being so absorbing as to suspend time. "Temporarily suspended from all normal external and internal activity while it is in these states of union, the soul is absorbed into the immediate presence of God,"[39] a presence which begins to transform the soul.

So transformative are these encounters that Teresa's primary metaphor in this dwelling place is the caterpillar to cocoon to butterfly. This metaphor of metamorphosis is an attempt to convey how

> the soul is beginning, through the moments of unitive encounter, to share in the essence of God by participation, causing a transformation of personhood. The center of the soul where these exchanges between God and the soul occur is being made into the very dwelling place of God, and God is becoming the very dwelling place of the soul.[40]

The soul emerges from such encounters changed. Thus, the butterfly

---

37. IC V:1:2; see below.
38. Henri Nouwen, *Life of the Beloved* (New York: Crossroad, 1992), 53–54.
39. Ahlgren, *Entering*, 66.
40. Ibid., 67.

represents a newly emerging relational self. To use more technical language, in this stage, the human person is now consciously theonomous—that is, she names herself "with reference to her origin and destiny in God,"[41] and doubly empowered through the divine working in and with her. As I developed this idea of a shift from selfhood to relational personhood, I suggested that the soul's "new relational identity, then, represents a way of being with God, in an intersubjective relationship that it could not have supported in its previous state of selfhood. In this identity it does not cease to be itself, yet its very selfhood has been transformed as a result of its relational identity."[42]

Part of what Teresa captures here is the transforming power of love, which is to say, the transforming power of God—a power that transforms us even as it invites us into a new way of being connected, constantly, to God. As we avail ourselves of that power, we are empowered to share it with others.

Passages from Teresa's Fifth Dwelling Places

How can I explain the riches and treasures and delights found in the fifth dwelling places? I believe it would be better not to say anything about these remaining rooms, for there is no way of learning how to speak of them; neither is the intellect capable of understanding them, nor do comparisons serve much in explaining them, because earthly things are rather base for this end. (IC V:1:1)

So, my sisters, since in some ways we can delight in heaven on earth, be brave in asking God to give us God's favor so that nothing will be lacking for our fault, and that God might show us the way and strengthen the soul so that it can dig until it finds this hidden

---

41. See Catherine Mowry LaCugna, *God for Us: The Trinity and Christian Life* (New York: Harper Collins, 1991), 290. See development of this idea in Ahlgren, *Entering*, 68–72.

42. Ahlgren, *Entering*, 68. As I note there, this is a realization of what Denys Turner has identified as the foundation of mystical theology when he writes: "We begin to glimpse what union with God can mean, and equally what true human identity can be, only when the languages of both [personal identity and union] are pushed to the limit and are there *held together*." See Denys Turner, *Eros and Allegory*, (Kalamazoo, MI: Cistercian Publications, 1995), 61 (emphasis his).

treasure,[43] since it is true that it is within us. This is what I would like to explain, if the Lord will enable me to do. (IC V:1:2)

I said "strengthen the soul," so that you will understand that bodily strength is not necessary in this, especially if God does not grant it to us; God would never make it impossible for someone to arrive at the riches God grants. Indeed, God is happy simply in seeing each one do what is in her. Blessed be such a great God! And so, see, daughters, that in what we are talking about, God wants you to hold nothing back. Whether you have little or much, God wants all for Godself, and in conformity with what you have given of yourselves you will be given greater or lesser favors. There is no greater proof for seeing whether or not our prayer has arrived at union or not. Do not think that this union is like a dream, . . . even though it seems like the soul is asleep. It is not really asleep, nor does it feel awake. But it is completely "asleep" to the things of this world and even to ourselves, because it remains as if without the use of its senses for however long this prayer lasts, and it cannot actively think, even if it wanted to. Here there is no need for any kind of technique to suspend its thought. (IC V:1:3)

As for love, if it does love, it does not understand how, nor even what it is that it loves. Nor would it even want to; in sum, it is, in everything, like someone who has died to the world, in order to live more fully in God. And thus it is a delightful kind of death, an uprooting of the soul from all of the operations that it might have while it lives in the body. And this is delightful because it actually seems that the soul leaves the body in order to dwell more perfectly in God, in such a way that I don't even know if there remains enough life in it to breathe. (Now that I think about it, it almost seems that it doesn't; at least, if it does, it is not aware of it.) It wants to employ all of its understanding in understanding something of what it is experiencing, and since it is unable to do that, it remains full of wonder, in such a way that it is either totally lost to itself or at least neither a foot nor a hand stirs, just as we say here of a person who is so unconscious that they seem dead to us. Oh, secrets of God! I would never tire of trying to explain them

43. Cf. Matt. 13:44.

if I thought I could get something right! And so I shall say a thousand nonsensical things if only to get a few things right, so that we might praise God more. (IC V:1:3)

I said that this union was not like a dream because until the soul has a lot of experience in this dwelling place, it remains a little confused about what just happened to it: whether it has imagined it; whether it was asleep; whether the experience was a gift from God or whether the devil was transformed into an angel of light. So it is left with a thousand suspicions. And it is a good thing to have them, because, as I said, our own nature can deceive us sometimes, and even though there is not really much room for all of those poisonous things to enter here, some little lizards might; they are stubborn and pesky little things, and they can make their way into lots of places. And even though they do not cause harm here, especially if we don't pay any attention to them, as I said, since they can be a bother since they are little thoughts that proceed from the imagination. But here, for as keen as these lizards may be, they cannot enter this dwelling place, because there is neither imagination nor memory nor understanding that can impede this grace. And I will even dare to affirm that, if this is truly union with God, the devil cannot enter or do any harm, because His Majesty is so deeply joined and united to the essence of the soul that he does not dare approach, nor can he even really understand this secret. . . . Oh great good! State in which this accursed one does us no harm! And thus the soul is left with such great blessings which God has worked in her, without anyone impeding Him, not even ourselves. What will God not give us, who is so fond of giving and who can give all that He wants? (IC V:1:4)

This union is above all earthly joys, above all delights, above all consolations, and still more than that. It doesn't matter where those spiritual or earthly joys come from, for the feeling they engender is very different, as you will have experienced. I once said[44] that the difference is like that between feeling something on the rough outer

44. See Teresa's *Meditations on the Song of Songs* 4:2.

covering of the body or in the marrow of the bones. And that was right on the mark, for I don't know how to say it better. (IC V:1:5)

Now I want to tell you of a clear sign by which you will be sure not to be deceived nor to have doubts that this has come from God; His Majesty brought it to mind today, and, to my way of seeing, it is the sure sign. . . . And it is that you see that God has made this soul a fool with regard to all things, so as better to seal upon her true wisdom. She neither sees nor hears nor understands during the time that she is in this state, which is always short (and it seems to her even shorter that what it must be)—and in this space God adheres Godself in the interior of that soul, in such a way that, when the soul returns to itself, it can in no way doubt that it was in God and God was in it. This truth remains with it so firmly that, even if years pass without God granting her this favor again, she cannot forget it nor can she doubt that it happened. And this is without taking into account all of the effects that remain in her afterward, which I will tell you about later. For this is what matters most. (IC V:1:6)

***

Now I recall, in what I say about our not having a part to play [in bringing about this union], what you have heard the Bride say in the Song of Songs: "The king brought me into the wine cellar . . ." or "he placed me there," I think it says.[45] And it doesn't say she went. And it also says that she went looking for her Beloved all over the place.[46] I understand this union to be the wine cellar where the Lord wishes to place us when He desires and as He desires. And however great the effort we make to do so, we ourselves cannot enter. God must place us there and then God enters as well into the center of our soul . . . just as [Christ] entered the place where his disciples were and greeted them saying "peace be with you"[47] and left the tomb without opening the stone. Further on you will see in the final dwelling place how God

45. Song of Songs 1:4.
46. See Song of Songs 2:4, 3:2.
47. John 20:19.

desires that the soul enjoy God in her very own center, even much more than here. (IC V:1:11)

***

It will seem to you that I have said all that there is to say about this dwelling place. But there is much more, since, as I have said, there are many degrees of intensity to this union. I don't know that I will know how to say more, except that when souls to whom God grants all these favors prepare themselves, there are many things to say about what God works in them. I will speak of some of them and of their effects on the soul. And to explain them better, I want to make use of a comparison which is very good for this purpose, and also that we may see how, even though in this work that the Lord does, we can do nothing, still there is a lot to dispose ourselves so that God might grant us this favor. (IC V:2:1)

You must already have heard about God's marvels manifested in the way silk originates, for only God could have invented something like that. The silkworms come from seeds about the size of little grains of pepper. . . . When the warm weather comes and the leaves begin to appear on the mulberry tree, the seeds start to live, for they are dead until then. The worms nourish themselves on the mulberry leaves until, having grown to full size, they settle on some twigs. There with their little mouths they themselves go about spinning the silk and making some very thick little cocoons in which they enclose themselves. The silkworm, which is fat and ugly, then dies, and a little white butterfly, which is very pretty, comes forth from the cocoon. Now if this were not seen but recounted to us as having happened in other times, who would believe it? Or what reasonings could make us conclude that a thing as nonrational as a worm could be so diligent in working for our benefit and with so much industriousness? (IV V:2:2)

The silkworm starts to live when by the heat of the Holy Spirit it begins to benefit through the general help given to us all by God . . . by reading good books, and hearing sermons . . . and other things the soul can make use of. It then begins to live and sustain itself by these things, and by good meditations, until it is grown. Its being grown is what is relevant to what I'm saying. (IC V:2:3)

Well, once this silkworm is grown . . . it begins to spin the silk and build the house wherein it will die. I would like to point out here that this house is Christ. Somewhere, it seems to me, I have read or heard that our life is hidden in Christ or in God or that our life is Christ.[48] (IC V:2:4)

Well, see here, what we can do through the help of God: God Godself becomes our dwelling place, one that we build through this prayer of union. It seems I'm saying that we can build up God and take God away since I say that God is the dwelling place and we can build it in order to place ourselves in it. And, indeed, we can! Not that we can take God away or build God up, but we can take away from ourselves and build up, as do these little silkworms. For we will not have finished doing all that we can in this work when, to the little we do, which is nothing, God will unite Godself, with all God's greatness, and give the soul such high value that God Godself will become the reward of this work. (IC V:2:5)

Therefore let us have courage and be quick to do this work and weave this little cocoon by taking away our self-love and self-will. . . . And let this silkworm die, as it does in completing what it was created to do! . . . For when the soul is, in this prayer [of union], truly dead to the world, a little white butterfly comes forth. O greatness of God! How transformed the soul is when it comes out of this prayer after having been placed within the greatness of God and so closely joined with God for a little while. . . . Truly I tell you, the soul doesn't recognize itself. (IC V:2:6–7)

But to see the restlessness of this little butterfly, even though it has never been quieter and calmer in its life, is something for which we should praise God! For now it does not know where to alight and rest. For now that it has known such rest, everything that it sees on earth displeases it, especially when God gives it this wine often. With each of these encounters it gains new treasures. Now it holds as nothing the works it did while it was a caterpillar, which was to weave its cocoon

48. Col. 3:3–4.

little by little. Now it has wings, so how can it be happy walking step by step when it can fly? On account of its desires, everything it can do for God becomes little in its own eyes. (IC V:2:8)

I don't mean to say that those who arrive here do not have peace; they do have it, and it is very deep . . . But it grieves, too. For, like the bride in the Song of Songs, it desires most earnestly to be united with her Spouse; and the grief [of separation between encounters of God in prayer] reaches the intimate depth of our being. It seems that the pain breaks and grinds the soul into pieces. It is the same desire as Our Lord had at the Last Supper: "I have earnestly desired."[49] (IC V:2:10, 11, 13)

***

Well, let us turn to our little dove and let's see something of what God gives it in this state. It must always be understood that one has to strive to go forward in the service of God and in self-knowledge. And if it does nothing more than receive this favor and if, thinking that it already possesses a sure thing, it begins to become careless in its way of life and turns aside from the path to heaven, which are the commandments, the same thing will happen to it as happens to the caterpillar: it will give forth its seeds, so that other silkworms are produced, and it itself will die forever. I say that it will give forth its seeds because I hold that God's desire is that such a great favor not be given in vain. And thus, even if the soul itself does not benefit from it, at least it will benefit others. For since the soul is left with these desires and virtues [to make manifest its love of God by bringing other souls to God], it always brings benefits to other souls, and from its fervor, others will gain fervor. And even if it loses that fire, it still remains with the hope that others might benefit, and it enjoys showing them the favors that God grants to those who love and serve God. (IC V:3:1)

God asks just two things from us: love of God and love of neighbor. These are what we must work for. By keeping them with perfection, we do God's will and so we will be united with God. (IC V:3:7)

49. Luke 22:15.

We cannot know whether or not we love God, although there are strong indications for recognizing that we do; but we can know whether we love our neighbor. And be certain that the more advanced you see you are in love for your neighbor the more advanced you are in the love of God, for the love that God has for us is so great that to repay us for our love of neighbor, God will in a thousand ways increase the love we have for God. I cannot doubt this. (IC V:3:8)

***

It seems that the union has not reached the stage of spiritual betrothal. Here on earth, when two people are to be engaged, they talk about if they are in agreement and if they love one another, and they even go to see one another, so that each becomes more satisfied with the other. So, too, in this union with God, now that the agreement between the two has been made and this soul is well informed about the goodness of her Spouse, and so she also is determined to do in all things the will of her Spouse and anything that she sees will make Him happy. And His Majesty, as one who well understands that this is so, is already very pleased with her, and so God grants her this favor: since God wants her to understand Him better and, as they say, meet together in person and be joined together. We can say that this happens here, and it occurs in a very short time, in which there is not any exchange of gifts or favors but the soul sees, in a very secret way, who this Spouse is that she is going to marry. Her senses and faculties in no way could understand what is given to her to see in this short moment; but, God being God, this moment of sight leaves her far more worthy for the joining of hands, as they say, because the soul remains so in love that she now does everything in her power so that this divine betrothal might take place. (IC V:4:4)

Love is never idle, and such a failure would be a very bad sign. A soul that is chosen to be the betrothed of God and that is now intimate with God, and has reached the boundaries [that stretch directly into God] must not go to sleep. (IC V:4:10)

Sixth Dwelling Places

Prefatory Comment to Teresa:

The material Teresa covers in the sixth dwelling places, which is the space of final preparation for the fruition of union with God, is complicated and dense, but, as I have suggested previously, none of it is superfluous.[50] Rather, Teresa here chronicles how our deepening experiences of union with God gradually accomplish in us a new form of personhood. Simply put, there is a transformation in our very personhood that is being worked in us over time, as we are slowly transformed into the Lover who loves us into new life.[51] And as Teresa helps us to understand this experientially, we begin to know God as a lover. What is more, we begin to know God as relational activity. God is not simply an entity who wants to be in relationship with us. God is also a dynamic being who invites us into relationship-building in the world that God has created. By teaching us what it is to be in relationship, God gives us a new way of being—a new way of being ourselves, a new way of being human, a new way of being a part of the human community and a part of the web of creation. Naturally, such a way of being cannot be learned overnight, nor can it be accomplished in a moment. But perhaps, it can be accomplished moment by moment, once we are fully dedicated to the only relationship that has the infinite capacity to teach us both who we are and who we can become.

The process I am describing is possible only with rigorous, even total, self-dedication—what Teresa has called "a great and very determined determination" of the will.[52] While, in theory, all of us are

---

50. See Ahlgren, *Entering*, 79–82.
51. Cf. John of the Cross, "Dark Night," stanza 5.
52. See WP 21:2: "Turning to those who want to engage this journey and not stop until the end, which is to drink of this water of life, and how they must begin, I say that it is very important, in fact all-important—that they have a great and very determined determination not to stop until they arrive at the end, no matter who comes their way, whatever happens, whatever trials they must pass through, whoever murmurs against them, whoever arrives there, whoever dies on the road or does not have the heart for the trials that there are on it, even if the world drowns—as they so often say to us: "There are dangers there," "So-and-so lost her way here," "That one was deceived," "That one, even though she prayed a lot, got tripped up," "They lose their virtue," "It's not for women, since they can become delusional," "Better that they stick to their spinning,"

capable of it, clearly, many—if not most of us—will begin to suffer from "cold feet." A relational identity, especially in a world as confused, careless, twisted, and even violent as ours is, must be approached with caution, wisdom, and maturity. Perhaps it is, in some ways, a self-selecting vocation. And yet, it is ultimately the vocation of each Christian. And, as Teresa teaches here, the relational identity taught to us by Love Personified that corresponds to the reality that we are created in love and for love, is a path of intense grace, in which we are bathed in a transforming love that completely undoes us. It is a journey that each of us must undertake as individuals, because ultimately, each of us must make the journey according to the unique contours of our life-with-God; yet, it is also a journey that would be impossible to make without support and companions concurrently committed to this journey.

All of this, Teresa covers in the sixth dwelling places, the space where we now learn to hold nothing back from God and become totally absorbed in the growing and intensifying relationship that God and we both desire. For "now the soul is determined to take no other spouse."[53]

Passages from Teresa's Sixth Dwelling Places:

Well, then, let us, with the help of the Holy Spirit, speak of the sixth dwelling places, where the soul is now wounded with love for its Spouse and strives for more opportunities to be alone and, in conformity with its state, to rid itself of everything that can be an obstacle to this solitude. That time together[54] is so engraved in the soul that its whole desire is only to enjoy it again. Now the soul is fully determined to take no other spouse. But the Spouse does not look at the soul's great desires that the betrothal take place, for God still wants it to desire this more; the betrothal takes place at a cost; it is the greatest of blessings. (IC VI:1:1)

God help me, what interior and exterior trials the soul suffers before

---

"Such complicated things are not necessary," or "Praying the Our Father and the Hail Mary is quite enough."

53. IC VI:1:1
54. Here, Teresa is referring to the prayer of union described in IC V:4:4.

entering the seventh dwelling places! (IC VI:1:1) I believe it will be well to recount some of these trials that I know one will certainly undergo. (IC VI:1:2) There is an outcry by persons who know her and even those who don't . . . gossip like the following: "She's trying to make out she's a saint; she goes to extremes to deceive the world and bring others to ruin; there are others better Christians who don't put on all this outward show." (And it's worth nothing that she is not putting on any outward show but just striving to fulfill well her state in life.) Those she considered her friends turn away from her, and they are the ones who take the largest and most painful bite at her: "That soul has gone astray and is clearly mistaken; these are things of the devil; she has deceived her confessors . . ." (IC VI:1:3)

You will tell me that there are also those who will speak well of that soul . . . But praise is just another trial greater than those mentioned! Since the soul sees clearly that if it has anything good this is given by God and is by no means its own, praise is an intolerable burden to it, at least in the beginning. When the soul reaches the stage at which it pays little attention to praise, it pays much less to disapproval; on the contrary, it rejoices in this, for blame does not intimidate the soul but strengthens it. (IC VI:1:4–5)

There is also the torment of confessors who have little experience. They fear everything and find in everything something to doubt because of such unusual experiences. They become especially doubtful if they notice some imperfection in a soul that has them, for it seems to such confessors that the ones to whom God grants great favors must be angels—but that is impossible as long as they are in this body. Everything is immediately condemned as from the devil or melancholy. The poor soul that walks with fear and goes to its confessor as to its judge, and is condemned by him, cannot help but be deeply tormented and disturbed. (IC VI:1:8)

In sum, there is no remedy in this tempest but to wait for the mercy of God. For at an unexpected time, with one word alone or a chance happening, God so quickly calms the storm that it seems that there had not been even as much as a cloud in that soul, and it remains filled with sunlight and much more consolation. (IC VI:1:10) The best remedy, in the meantime, is to engage in external works of charity and to hope in the mercy of God, who never fails those who have hope in Him. (IC VI:1:13)

Now let us begin to discuss the way that the Spouse has with the soul and how before God belongs to it completely God makes it desire God vehemently by certain delicate means that the soul itself does not understand. (Nor do I believe I'll be successful in explaining them save to those who have experienced them.) Because these are impulses so delicate and refined that they proceed from very deep within the interior part of the soul, I don't know any comparison that will fit. (IC VI:2:1)

They are far different from all that we can acquire of ourselves here below and even from the spiritual delights that were mentioned. . . . It [the soul] is made to tremble and even complain without there being anything that causes it pain. It feels that it is wounded in the most delightful way, but it doesn't learn how or by whom it was wounded. It knows clearly that the wound is something precious, and it would never want to be cured. (IC VI:2:2)

I am struggling to explain for you this action of love, and I don't know how. For it seems a contradiction that the Beloved would give the soul clear understanding that God is with it and yet also make it think that God is calling it by a sign so certain that no room is left for doubt and a whisper so penetrating that the soul cannot help but hear it . . . and this action of love is so powerful that the soul dissolves with desire, and yet it doesn't know what to ask for since clearly it thinks that its God is with it. (IC VI:2:3–4)

What greater good does it want? I don't know . . . I was thinking now that it's as though from this fire enkindled in my God, the Source of all fire, a spark leapt forth and so struck the soul that it felt the flaming fire. And since the spark was not yet enough to set the soul on fire itself, and the fire is so delightful, the soul is left with that pain. Merely by touching the soul, the spark produces such an effect. (IC VI:2:4)

Here there is no reason to wonder whether the experience is

brought on naturally or caused by melancholy, or whether it is some trick of the devil or some illusion. It is something that leaves clear understanding of how this activity comes from the place where the Lord, who is unchanging, dwells. (IC VI:2:5)

God also has other ways of awakening the soul: unexpectedly when it is praying vocally and without thinking of anything interior, it seems a delightful enkindling will come upon it as though a fragrance were suddenly to become so powerful as to spread through all the senses. Or the experience is something like this, and it is communicated only for the sake of making one feel the Spouse's presence there. It moves the soul to a delightful desire of enjoying God, and thus the soul is prepared to make intense acts of love and praise of our Lord. (IC VI:2:8)

God has another way of awakening the soul and, even though in some ways it seems to be a greater favor than the ones mentioned it can be more dangerous; for that reason I shall spend more time on it. There are many kinds of locutions given to the soul: some seem to come from outside it, others from the very interior of the soul, others from the superior part of it, and others are so external that they are heard with the ears, for they seem to come from a formed voice . . . (IC VI:3:1)

All the kinds I mentioned can be from God or from the devil or from one's own imagination. I will say, if I can, with the favor of God, the signs there are in these differences. . . . (IC VI:3:4)

Whether they come from the interior, the superior or the exterior, that does not matter in determining if they come from God. The surest signs they are from God that can be had, in my opinion, are these: the first and truest is the power and authority they bear, for locutions from God effect what they say. Let me say more: a soul finds itself in the midst of all the tribulation and inner disturbance that was mentioned, and in darkness of the intellect and in dryness; then, with one word alone of these that the Lord says ("don't be distressed"), it is left calm and free from all distress, with great light, and without all that suffering. And even if the entire world and all kinds of learned people came together to give reasons why she should not be distressed, with all of their work they would never have been able to ride her of that affliction. . . . But then, with that one word that she was told, "It is I; do not be afraid," she was immediately unafraid and even remained greatly consoled, and knew that she could never be convinced otherwise. (IC VI:3:5)

The second sign is the great quiet left in the soul, the devout and peaceful recollection, the readiness to engage in the praises of God. (IC VI:3:6)

The third sign is that these words remain in the memory for a very long time, and some are never forgotten, as are those we hear on earth . . . . The locution takes place in such intimate depths and a person with the ears of the soul seems to hear those words from the Lord so clearly and so in secret that this very way in which they are heard, together with the acts that the vision itself produces, assures that person and gives certitude that the devil can have no part to play in the locution. (IC VI:3:7)

Since I have spoken to many spiritual people, I want to write down here some of the ways that I have understood that God gives raptures . . . . (IC VI:4:2)

One way is that, the soul, even though not in prayer, is touched by some word that it remembers or hears from God, and then it seems that His Majesty, from the interior of the soul, makes the flame that we spoke of[55] grow, moved with pity to see the soul suffer this desire for so long. All burnt up, like a phoenix, she remains renewed and can devoutly believe that she is pardoned of all her faults—this must be understood with the disposition and means that the soul has had, as the Church teaches—and thus cleansed, God joins her to Godself, without anyone being able to understand this but the two of them. The soul herself understands this in a way that she can explain later, although she is not without interior sense, for this is not like someone fainting or having a fit, when nothing, inside or out, is understood. (IC VI:4:3)

What I know in this case is that the soul has never been so attuned

---

55. See IC VI:2:4.

to the things of God nor had such great light and understanding of His Majesty. (IC VI:4:4)

When the soul is in this suspension, the Lord is pleased to show her some secrets, about heavenly things and imaginary visions, and she is able to speak of them afterward, for they remain so impressed on the memory that they are never forgotten. But when the visions are intellectual, the soul does not know how to speak of them. (IC VI:4:5)

There is another rapture or flight of the spirit, as I call it—that, though it is of the same substance, the interior feels it very differently—in which suddenly sometimes one feels a movement in the soul that is so swift that it seems that its spirit is swept away with a velocity that almost frightens it, especially at the beginning. This is why I was telling you that great courage is necessary for the ones to whom God is going to grant these favors—and even faith and confidence and a great openness that God may do with the soul whatever God wants. Do you think it is only a minor disturbance for a person to be very much in her senses and yet to see her soul completely drawn out of her? And sometimes even the body along with it, as I have read? And all of this without knowing where it is going, what or who is taking it or how? Because at the beginning of this swift movement, there is not so much certainty that all of this comes from God. (IC VI:5:1)

Then again, is there any real solution in trying to resist? No way; indeed, that is even worse. I know of a person to whom it seemed that God wanted to show that the soul that has so earnestly placed itself in God's hands, offering God everything with complete willingness, now has nothing more to do. In fact, that soul [who gives itself over so completely] is carried off with even more impetuous movement. And so it decided not to do anything more than a piece of straw when drawn by the amber, if you have noticed that, and leave itself in the hands of the One who is so powerful, for it see that it is best to make a virtue of necessity. (IC VI:5:2)

For now it seems that that fountain of water that we spoke of—I believe in the fourth dwelling places, but I don't remember too well[56]—filled itself with such great gentleness and quiet—or without any real movement, I mean. But here it seems that this great God, who holds back the springs of water and does not allow the sea to move beyond its boundaries, lets loose the springs which supply the water to this fountain; and with a great force, large and powerful waves raise up the little boat of our soul. And just as a little boat is not strong enough, nor is the pilot powerful enough to handle the boat when the waves arrive with intense fury, and thus it is tossed about wherever they send it, even less can the interior of the soul stay where it will or make its senses and faculties do anything more than what they are commanded. (IC VI:5:3) And so in this respect too, great courage is necessary, for this favor can frighten us, and, if our Lord did not give us courage, we might walk around afflicted. (IC VI:5:5)

The experience, quite obviously, is not from the devil, and it would certainly be quite impossible from our own imaginations, nor could the devil do something that ends up leaving such peace and rest in the soul. For three things, especially, are left in the soul to a very sublime degree: knowledge of the grandeur of God, since the more things we see of that grandeur, the more we can understand of it; self-knowledge and humility at seeing how a small thing as we are in comparison with the Creator of such greatness has dared to offend God and now does not dare to look toward God; and the third: to esteem very little all the things of the world except in so far as they can be placed in the service of such a great God. (IC VI:5:10)

These are the jewels that the Spouse begins to give the betrothed, and they are of such great value that the soul will not want to lose them. And thus these meetings, too, remain engraved in the memory, and I believe it is impossible to forget them until we enjoy them forever—unless this be for some grave fault. But the Spouse who gives them is powerful enough to give the soul the grace not to lose them. (IC VI:5:11)

***

56. See IC IV:2:2.

Further Comment on the Sixth Dwelling Places:

If we take a moment now to reflect on the material contained in the first half of the sixth dwelling places, we see there a catalog of experiences of intimacy with God—all of which leave a residual effect on the soul. Teresa speaks of loving communications which sear their way into the soul and remain within, embedding their way into our consciousness, and gradually transforming the inner reality of the human person. The relational identity we began to speak of in the fifth dwelling places is now becoming more intensely realized. Additionally, in their aggregate, these intimate encounters with God leave the soul both prepared for and longing more deeply for a full consummation of the union with God that each encounter promises. All of what we have read so far parallels John of the Cross' material from the end of the *Dark Night*, where the soul is "enkindled" with an "infused love."[57]

This enkindling produces a profound longing, which Teresa develops in chapter six of the sixth dwelling places, and the subsequent chapters (7–11) describe the turn toward intimate union with God that a companionate relationship with Christ cements. Here, as Teresa chronicles for us, God incarnate, known to us by means of Christ's constant presence in and through our humanity, leads us to deeper, more permanent knowledge of God. "Repeated experiences of Christ's presence stimulate the soul's constant recollection of the incarnate God, which, in turn, reinforces the soul's knowledge of its essential nature in God."[58]

Further Passages from Teresa's Sixth Dwelling Places:

As a result of these great favors, the soul remains full of longings to enjoy completely the One who has granted them. And thus it lives with real torment, even though this is delightful. It feels great yearnings to die, and so it often asks God, with tears, to take it from this exile. Everything it sees wearies it. When it is alone, it has some relief, but

57. See DN II:11:1–7, below, pp. 91–4.
58. Ahlgren, *Entering*, p. 107.

soon this sorrow returns; and when the soul does not feel it, it feels something missing. In sum, this little butterfly now finds no lasting place to rest. Rather, because love has made the soul so tender, whatever occasion there may be to enkindle more this flame makes it fly, and thus, in this dwelling place, the raptures are almost continual, without there being any real way to avoid them, even if they are public. And then come criticism and persecutions that, even though she would prefer to be without any care at all, no one leaves her alone, because many people harass her, especially confessors. (IC VI:6:1)

In the midst of these hard yet delightful things, Our Lord sometimes gives the soul intense joys and a kind of strange prayer that the soul does not recognize. And I tell you this in case God gives you this favor, so that you will know what is happening and praise God greatly. This prayer is, it seems to me, a kind of great union of the soul's faculties, and then God leaves them with total freedom to enjoy this delight. And the same is true with the senses, although they do not know exactly what they are enjoying or how they are enjoying it. What I am describing may seem like gibberish, but it does seem to happen this way, so that the joy that the soul feels is so excessive that it is impossible to enjoy it alone, and therefore she wants to share it with others, so that they, too, will join her in praising God—for that is the true end of all of her inclinations. Oh, the festivities and celebrations she would arrange, so that all could understand and share her joy! It is as if she has found herself and, like the father of the prodigal son,[59] she would want to invite everyone to a great feast now that she sees her soul placed in a space where she cannot doubt that it is safe, at least for the moment. And I believe that this is truly so, because she enjoys such interior joy in the very intimate part of the soul and such peace, and all of her joy provokes great praises of God; this kind of experience is not possible for the devil to give us. (IC VI:6:10)

I would want you, sisters, to pray in this way often, with praises that rise from the interior of your souls, for the one who gets this kind of prayer started can awaken all the others. (IC VI:6:12)

59. See Luke 15:22.

It will seem to you that whoever enjoys such lofty things will no longer meditate on the mysteries of the most sacred humanity of our Lord Jesus Christ, since she is now perfectly engaged in loving.[60] This is something I wrote about at length in another place,[61] and even though they have criticized me for it and have said that I do not understand this well—for they say that these are paths along which Our Lord leads and that, once they have passed beyond the beginning stages, it is better to engage the divinity of God directly and let go of corporeal things—they will never convince me that such a path is a good one. Now, it could be that I am mistaken and we are all saying the same thing. But I saw quite well that the devil himself was trying to deceive me in that way, and therefore I have so learned my lesson from experience that I think that, even though I have said it many times, I will say it another time here, so that you will be well advised. And note that I dare say that you should not believe anyone who tells you something else. And I will try to explain more what I wrote in that other place. I don't know if someone has written down what I was told once, since it would be good to explain this matter at length, and put all of it together, since confusion on this can do a lot damage for those who do not understand very well. (IC VI:7:5)

It may also seem to some people that they cannot think [any more] about the Passion or even less about the Blessed Virgin or the lives of the saints, even though remembering them can bring such great benefit and new life. I cannot imagine what they are thinking. To be separated from our bodies and always enkindled in love is for angelic spirits, not of those of us who live in mortal bodies. In fact it is necessary for us to speak to, think about, and be good companions to those who, also having had mortal bodies, did such great deeds for God. How much more necessary it is not to withdraw deliberately from all of our good and help, which is the most sacred humanity of Our Lord Jesus Christ. I cannot believe that people do this, unless they simply

---

60. Teresa's language here, "se ejercitará ya toda en amor," is the same as John's in SC 328, "que ya solo en amar es mi ejercicio."
61. Here, Teresa refers to chapter 22 of her *Life*, now confiscated by the Spanish Inquisition and therefore inaccessible.

don't understand, but still they harm themselves and others in doing so. At the very least, I can assure them that they will not enter these last two dwelling places, because, if they lose their guide, who is our good Jesus, they will not know the way. In fact, it will be quite a feat for them to be safely in the other dwelling places, since Christ says that He is the way[62] and indeed the Lord says that He is light[63] and that no one can come to God without Him, and that "whoever sees me, sees God."[64] Others will argue that these words mean something else. I don't know about those "other meanings." I have gotten along very well with this meaning that my soul has always felt to be true. (IC IV:7:6)

There are some souls—and many of them have come to talk with me about this—who, after Our Lord has brought them to perfect contemplation, would like to remain in that state always. This cannot be. But God does grant this grace: afterward they cannot engage discursive meditation on the life and passion of Christ as they did before, and I don't know why. But this is very common: the understanding is now less inclined and even less capable of meditation. I believe that the reason for this is that, since meditation is all about seeking God and now that they have found God, the soul grows more accustomed to using the will to seek God rather than tiring itself out by using the intellect. Besides, the will is now enkindled, and this more generous faculty does not want to use the intellect if it doesn't have to. This is not a bad thing. In fact, it would be impossible, especially for arriving at the final dwelling places, to use the intellect, and it would be a waste of time, although many times it needs the help of the intellect in order for the will to be enkindled. (IC VI:7:7)

And note this point, sisters, since it is important, and therefore I want to say something else: the soul desires to be completely occupied in love; it would not want to be taken up by anything else. Indeed, it will not be able to, even if it wanted to. Although the will is not dead, the fire that usually makes it burn is dying out, and it is necessary for someone to blow on it in order to help it give off heat . . . (IC VI:7:8) Now

62. John 14:6.
63. John 8:12.
64. John 14:6, 9.

the soul whom God places in the seventh dwelling places rarely or even never has to worry about this. . . . For that person walks continually in an admirable way with Christ our Lord, in whom the divine and the human are joined, and who is now always in that person's company. Therefore, when the flame in the will is not enkindled and we do not feel God's presence, it is necessary for us to seek out this presence [of Christ]. That is what God wants, just as the bride in the Song of Songs did.[65] (IC VI:7:9)

Nor is it possible that the soul forget that it has received so much from God, so many signs of such precious love, because these are living sparks that will enkindle it more in the love that it has for God. (IC VI:7:11)

So that you will see, sisters, that what I have told you is true and that the farther along a soul progresses, the more accompanied by this good Jesus it finds itself, it would be good for me to speak about how, when God wants, we cannot do otherwise than walk always with Christ. In this way, you will see clearly the ways and manners that God communicates Godself to us and shows us the love God has for us. For God gives us admirable visions and even some apparitions, and, if God grants you this favor I would not want you to be too overwhelmed. I hope that God be served that I may explain well something of these, so that we might praise God all the more. And even if God does not grant them to us, we should still praise God who, although filled with majesty and power, nonetheless desires to communicate so directly with a creature. (IC VI:8:1)

It happens that, when a soul is least expecting that such a favor may be granted to it and not having thought she might merit it, will feel Our Lord Jesus Christ next to her, even though she does not see him with the eyes of either her body or her soul. They call this an "intellectual vision," although I do not know why. I saw this person to whom God granted this favor (and other favors that I will speak of later) quite worried at the beginning, because she did not know what exactly was happening, nor did she see anything. However, she knew quite clearly

---

65. Song of Songs 3:3.

that this was Jesus Christ our Lord who was showing himself to her in a way she could not doubt; I mean she could not doubt that the sight of him was there. But as to whether or not this was of God, even though she felt such powerful effects that she understood that it was, she was nonetheless concerned. For she had never even heard of an "intellectual vision" nor did she think that there was such a thing, although she understood quite clearly that this was the same Lord who spoke to her so many times, in the way mentioned.[66] But until God granted her this favor that I am describing, she did not know who was speaking to her, although she understood the words. (IC VI:8:2)

I know that, being afraid of this vision—because it is not like one of those imaginary visions, which passes quickly; rather, this type lasts for many days, and even, once, for more than a year—she went to her confessor quite concerned. He said to her that if she couldn't see anything, how could she know that it was our Lord? And that she tell him what his face looked like.[67] She said that she did not know, that she had not seen the face, nor could she say anything more than what she had said. All that she knew was that this was the One who spoke with her and that this was no fancy on her part. And even though others were quite suspicious of this, she still could not doubt, especially when He said to her: "Do not be afraid; it is I."[68] Those words conveyed such strength that she could no longer doubt, and so she remained fortified and happy with such good company, since she clearly saw

---

66. In IC VI:8:3.

67. This is a recounting of the conversation first described in L 27:3–5. The vision may have taken place about the year 1560, when Teresa was still at the convent of the Encarnación, prior to the reform. Of this experience, she writes in L 27:10: "It seems to me that God wants the soul to have some awareness of what happens in heaven, and it seems to me that, just like there one understands without needing to speak (which I did not know for sure was like that until God, in God's goodness, wanted me to see and so God showed this to me in a rapture), so it is in this experience, since God and the soul understand one another, without words and with only the desire of God that the soul understands. And this is so that the soul might understand the deep love that is there between two closest friends. Just like here on earth when two people love each other very much and have a mutual understanding of one another: they seem to understand one another without words but only through their mutual regard. It must be that same way here: without our knowing how, these two lovers gaze upon one another, just as the Spouse says to the beloved in the Song of Songs [4:9: 'You have ravished my heart with one glance of your eyes']." Subsequent conversations with Peter of Alcántara helped Teresa to understand the nature of this experience and, in particular, to connect it to the tradition of intellectual visions. See L 27:3.

68. See L 25:18. Cf. Matt. 14:27, John 6:20, and Mark 6:50, spoken to the disciples as Jesus walked on the water.

what a great help it was to her to walk with a habitual remembrance of God and a great concern to avoid anything that might displease God. Now it seemed to her that God regarded her always, and every time she wanted to speak with God in prayer, and even outside of prayer, it seemed to her that God was so near that God could not fail to hear her. But she did not hear words whenever she wanted, but rather only suddenly and whenever they were necessary. (IC VI:8:3)

This favor brings with it a very particular knowledge of God. And this continual companionship gives rise to a most tender love for God and even greater desires to devote oneself completely to the service of God. It also brings a great purity of conscience, because the presence at its side makes the soul pay attention to everything. Even though we already know that God is present in all that we do, our nature is such that we neglect to think about this. But it is impossible not to forget that truth here, since God awakens it to the fact that God is right next to her. And the favors that have been described become quite common, because now the soul is walking around continually with true love for the One whom it sees and understands is always at her side. (IC VI:8:4)

In sum, this very great favor clearly gives the soul great gain, and so it should be highly valued. And the soul thanks God that she has been given it without being able to merit it in any way, and she would not exchange that blessing for anything in the world. And when the Lord is served to remove it from her, she feels great solitude; but no amount of effort on her part would be able to place her back in this company: God gives this sense of presence when God wants; it is not something that we can acquire for ourselves. (IC VI:8:5)

And so believe me that the safest way to proceed is in not wanting anything except what God wants, since God knows us far better than we know ourselves, and, besides that, God loves us! Let us place ourselves in God's hands that God's will be done in us, and then we will not err, especially if we maintain this disposition with a determined will. (IC VI:9:16)

For the desire of souls inflamed with love . . . is to satisfy love. And it is the nature of love to pour forth always in deeds. It would do so in a thousand ways, and, if it could, it would find a way for its soul to be totally consumed in love. (IC VI:9:18)

Here you will see, sisters, whether I was right in saying that courage is necessary, and whether, when you ask God for these favors, God is right in responding as to the sons of Zebedee: "Can you drink from this chalice?"[69] (IC VI:11:11)

Seventh Dwelling Places

Prefatory Comment to Teresa:

The seventh dwelling places concern the consummation of union between God and the soul. They reflect the full realization of an ontological partnership that has been gradually forged in the soul, primarily by God, but constantly with the soul's consent and participation. Several things are notable about how Teresa characterizes this union. First, although the language in the previous dwelling places, especially the sixth, has been christological, leading us to think that the union she is going to describe here will be with Christ, we find instead that the mystical life is fully realized not with one person of the Trinity, but as a participation in the Trinity. Christ has become a bridge for us to enter into that divine life, the perichoretic flow of love that makes the three persons one and that wants to flow out into all creation. And so, we participate in that loving activity. Here, the "restlessness of the butterfly" that has no place to settle[70] is resolved: no longer restless, the soul shares in the divine energy as it outpours and sustains that energy with a union that is there "whenever it takes notice."[71] Teresa speaks of the "divine breasts" through which "God is always sustaining the soul" and bringing it comfort. The soul dwells in the abundance of that energy which feeds its capacity to please God and offer others some portion of this abundance of love.

---

69. Matt. 20:22.
70. IC VI:2:8.
71. IC VII:1:9; cf. IC VII:2:4.

Teresa's insistence on the permanent apprehension of the Trinity (which reiterates the principle articulated by Augustine in his *On the Trinity*) embedded in the soul through the love of God is also noteworthy. It suggests that God is no longer experienced through the kinds of partial revelatory moments that characterized the sixth dwelling places. Rather, in the seventh dwelling places the presence of God is a normative, ongoing way of seeing and apprehending reality. Teresa uses the core text in the Christian mystical tradition to express this: 1 Cor. 6:17, where God and the soul have become "one in spirit," and while her teaching is entirely consistent with the tradition, it was one of the sorest points in posthumous criticisms of her works.[72] What is most striking about what Teresa accomplishes here is seamlessness, not only of the union between God and the soul, but of being and doing. God's indwelling presence and constant, loving activity are seamlessly present and active in the soul, who now learns to live in the dynamism of the Trinity.

Passages from Teresa's Seventh Dwelling Places

Here [in this seventh dwelling place] the union comes about in a different way: Our good God now desires to remove the scales from the soul's eyes so that it might see and understand, although in a strange way, something of the favor God grants it. When the soul is brought into that dwelling place, the Most Blessed Trinity, all three Persons, through an intellectual vision, is revealed to the soul through a certain representation of the truth. . . . It knows in such a way that what we hold by faith, it understands, we can say, through sight—although the sight is not with the bodily eyes nor with the eyes of the soul, because we are not dealing with an imaginative vision. Here all three Persons communicate themselves to it, speak to it, and explain those words of the Lord in the Gospel: that Christ and God and the Holy Spirit will come to dwell with the soul that loves God and keeps God's commandments.[73] (IC VII:1:6)

---

72. See discussion in *TAPS*, 126–33.
73. John 14:23.

And each day this soul is more amazed, for these persons never seem to leave it, but it clearly beholds that they are within it. In the extreme interior, in some place very deep within itself, the nature of which it doesn't know how to explain, because of a lack of learning, it perceives this divine company. (IC VII:1:7)

You may think that as a result the soul will be outside itself and so absorbed that it cannot understand anything. On the contrary, the soul is much more occupied than before with everything pertaining to the service of God, and once its duties are over it remains with that enjoyable company. (IC VII:1:8)

It should be understood that the soul does not carry about this presence so entirely—I mean, so clearly—as it manifests itself the first time or as in other times that God wants to give it this gift. For, if it did, it would be impossible for it to do anything else, or even live among other people. But even though it is not with quite as clear a light, every time it stops to take notice, it finds itself in this company. (IC VII:1:9)

The union [of the seventh dwelling places] is like what we have when rain falls from the sky into a river or fount; all is water, for the rain that fell from heaven cannot be divided or separated from the water of the river. Or it is like what we have when a little stream enters the sea, there is no means of separating the two. . . . Perhaps this is what Saint Paul means in saying *The one who is joined or united to God becomes one spirit with God*,[74] and is referring to this sovereign marriage, presupposing that His Majesty has brought the soul to it through union. And [Paul] also says *To me to live is Christ, and to die is to gain*[75]; and so it seems the soul here could say the same thing, because this is where the little butterfly that we spoke of before dies, and with great joy, because its life now is Christ. (IC VII:2:4–5)

For there are almost never any experiences of dryness or interior disturbance of the kind that was present at times in all the other dwelling places, but the soul is almost always in quiet. There is no fear that this sublime favor can be counterfeited by the devil, but the soul

74. 1 Cor. 6:17.
75. Phil. 1:21.

is wholly sure that the favor comes from God. . . . And so in this temple of God, in this God's dwelling place, God alone and the soul rejoice together in the deepest silence. (IC VII:3:10)

I repeat that it is critical not to place your foundation only in praying and contemplating, since, if you do not grow in virtues and exercise them always, you will remain dwarves. And please God that it be only a matter of not growing, for you already know that whoever does not increase, decreases. I hold that love, where present, cannot possibly be content with remaining the same. (IC VII:4:9)

Do you think that your very great humility and mortification, your service of others and great charity toward them, and your love of God is of small benefit? This fire of love in you enkindles the souls of others, and with every other virtue you will be always awakening them. Such service will not be small but very great and very pleasing to the Lord. (IC VII:4:14)

Once you get used to enjoying this castle, you will find rest in all things, even those involving much labor, for you will have the hope of returning to the castle, which no one can take from you. (IC Epilogue:2)

3

—————

John of the Cross

Prefatory Comment to John of the Cross

Readers of John's mystical poetry are immediately greeted by an ethereal sensuality that strikingly places longing and desire at the center of human existence. John's writings highlight the mutual delight that God and the soul take in one another. God's longing for us and our longing for God manifest themselves constantly in a certain discontent, restlessness, and deep searching for "something more"—something beyond which the person has yet experienced. One of John's greatest contributions is that he names that "more" clearly and plainly for us: we long for "more" because we are relational people who long for the genuine and thoroughly intimate partnership with God that makes us come alive.[1] And this is because our longing for

---

1. See Iain Matthew's beautiful development of this point in *The Impact of God*, 17: "His entire enterprise pounds along in a relentless quest: that this person should be filled with this God. Life remains dispersed till this God is at its centre. Whether or not she realizes it, the human person aches for such a union: 'It was to reach this that he created her in his image and likeness'; it is for this that we are 'always hungering, by our very nature, and by the gift of God'; 'nothing less' than this will 'satisfy the heart'. 'In short, it was for this goal of love that we were created'. In saying this, John is not merely analyzing the species. He is recognizing a real possibility. He sees this as a live issue, and feels 'sorrow and pity' where people ignore it; sorrow, pity, and a certain disbelief:

God is a response to a far deeper longing: God's longing for us. In fact, this is John's point of departure, as he writes in this critical passage from *The Living Flame of Love* that we will explore below, but that we should note here as a basic "credo": "In the first place it should be known that if a person is seeking God, far more is her Lover seeking her."[2] It is this longing for encounter, this delight and comfort in one another's presence, that permeates John's works and constitutes the core of his theological contribution. We are created for relationship with God, which brings so much "fullness" that John asks us to create as much space for it as possible.

John's thought revolves around three major poems and their commentary: "The Dark Night," the "Spiritual Canticle," and "The Living Flame of Love." The poetry reflects a progression of intensity in the love that God and the soul share, beginning with the theme of mystical encounter.[3] The "Dark Night" is a glorious poem describing, in the first person, the impulse of a soul to leave its "house"—all that it knows as safe and secure—in order to enter the dark night that unites it with its Beloved.[4] The poem is reminiscent and reflective of the layers of the Song of Songs that allude to mystical encounter between the human person and God. Its tone is celebratory—the night is "glad" as the lover hastens to find and meet her lover, and the final three stanzas describe their intimacy in terms of gentle caresses and a suspension of all else other than their union. The poem gave rise to two entire theological treatises, *The Ascent of Mount Carmel* and *The Dark Night*, and it is referred to in John's two other major theological works, *The Spiritual Canticle* and *The Living Flame of Love*. Because it captures and conveys the dynamic of spiritual encounter between God and the soul, and because this spiritual encounter is repeated in ever-deepening

'Oh souls created for this greatness and summoned to it—what are you doing?'" See below, pp. 112–13.

2. LF 3:28; see discussion below, pp. 119–21.

3. Some commentators recommend that beginners start with John's "Living Flame of Love." See Brian Pitman, "How to Read the Works of St. John of the Cross" in Peter Slattery, *St. John of the Cross: A Spirituality of Substance* (New York: Alba House, 1994), 45–66.

4. For clarity's sake, I refer to the poem, "The Dark Night" in quotation marks, in order to distinguish it from the full-length mystical treatise *The Dark Night*. The same is true for the "Spiritual Canticle," which exists as both a poem and a mystical treatise, and "The Living Flame of Love."

ways throughout the mystical life, the "Dark Night" becomes both the grounding and a familiar point of reference for the many stages of the mystical life.

In John's line-by-line exposition of the poem in *The Ascent of Mount Carmel*, we are introduced to early forms of purgation—darknesses and trials that we experience as we commit ourselves to an intentional life of virtue and spiritual growth. Generally speaking, this work is about the movement toward greater moral clarity and personal and spiritual integrity. While such movement is rooted, ultimately, in a committed love-relationship with God, the developmental stages explored in this treatise are early ones which revolve around moral behavior and spiritual discipline. In John's line-by-line exposition of the poem in *The Dark Night*, he covers those obstacles and "imperfections" that emerge more clearly for us as our efforts toward intimacy with God become more refined. The purgation described here is more profound, rooted in the cultivation not just of a good moral life, but in a growing intimacy with God—an intimacy that can only be explored when one has achieved an inner stability rooted in self-knowledge and an increased ability to access one's own spiritual gifts. Such a life depends upon both grace and an offering of "what is in us;" thus, John refers to the forms of purgation as both "active" and "passive," "sensual" and "spiritual." Ongoing references in his other mystical works, both to darkness and to spiritual intimacy, continue to open up dimensions of the illuminative and unitive life. If, as one intuits from the tone of the poem itself, it was composed spontaneously as an outpouring of love of God, John appears to have intended the poem to function quite systematically. He spent years after its original composition unpacking its content, working and reworking the prose commentary as a teaching tool for the Carmelite reform.

The *Spiritual Canticle* is a far more extended development of relational transformation. In stanza after stanza of colloquial dialogue between two lovers, a song of creative expression emerges, not unlike the "love-stirring breezes" that animate the lovers' exchanges. The communication between the two grows into a wordless communion in which the two drink one another in love, their beings mutually infused with a loving and transforming knowledge of the other. In this work, longing begins to give way to self-sharing, a mutual *entrega*, or self-offering, in which two become one by feeding one another, taking in nourishment and sustenance from the exchange. Fully thirty-one of the stanzas in the poem were fashioned from the horror of the prison cell in Toledo, as John relied absolutely on divine communion for sustenance under the most stark conditions.

In *The Living Flame of Love*, John reviews the purgative process he has outlined in *The Ascent of Mount Carmel* and *The Dark Night*, asking us to see this process from a different vantage point: the point at which a soul has been transformed by God's love and is now a living flame of that same divine fire of love. John emphasizes several things in the retrospective view of the purgative process:

First, the sufferings of purgation "cannot be exaggerated; they are but little less than the sufferings of purgatory." They completely "break" the inner person in order to remake us, piece by piece, into a person of intense fire and passion. The intensity of the soul's suffering, for John, is exemplified in Lamentations, in which Jeremiah cries out that "he has broken my bones" and "has set me in dark places as those who are dead forever." The soul in purgation finds itself completely and absolutely uprooted from all that it has previously known of itself. "He has turned my steps and paths upside down."[5]

Second, the source of this intense suffering is the incongruity and disparity of the soul and God and any incongruities within the soul itself. Thus, "contraries rise up at this time against contraries" and "One contrary when close to the other makes it more manifest." In this sense, the perfection of God "assails" the imperfection of the soul. The "flame" of God "is itself extremely loving," but the excessive dryness and hardness of the human will prevent it from seeing or feeling the actual tenderness of the flame. Thus, the love and tenderness of God must "expel the dryness and hardness," and this process, which emits

---

5. Cf. Lam. 3:1–9 and discussion in LF, 1: 21. And compare this "undoing" of the soul as it is remade in and with God to the catalog of experiences Teresa describes in the first half of the sixth dwelling places of the *Interior Castle*.

itself gently and tenderly from God, feels harsh and oppressive to the soul.

Third, in addition to being an extraordinarily difficult process of transformation, the process only reinforces, for the soul, its own misery and poverty. Although in the process, the soul will become illumined, softened, and infinitely tender, the process itself can feel excessive and severe. However, in the *Living Flame of Love*, John reassures us that God "prepares individuals by a purification more or less severe in accordance with the degree to which they will be raised;" thus, there is a corresponding compensation for the suffering of the soul, a suffering that emerges out of the soul's own intense longing, both for union and for the transformation it sees within itself through its growing life in and with God. It is a suffering, too, that reflects the reality that we so often inhibit God's action in us and in our lives, whether by gravitating to what is picayune and too small for us or by being afraid to risk what little we have for who we might become; these are issues that Teresa puts right out on the table in the third dwelling places as she looks at humanity through the foil of the "rich young man." For John, the simple remedy was "nada"—nothing. But far from nihilism, John's "nothing" is the space for God to become one with us.

John says that contemplation "must necessarily annihilate" the soul, "undoing" it by "putting it into darkness, dryness, conflict, and emptiness," and the darkness suffered by the soul is "profound, frightful and extremely painful."[6] However, John also tells us that the source of our suffering is not God, but "the soul's own weakness and imperfection," and he cites Ecclesiasticus in describing the struggles that we must all undergo, as human persons, to acquire true wisdom: "My soul wrestled for her [wisdom], and my entrails were disturbed in acquiring her; therefore shall I possess a good possession."[7] Further, the sufferings are present because of imperfections that remain in the soul; "once they are gone," John reminds us, "there is nothing

6. DN II: 9:2, 3.
7. Ecclus. 51:25, 29; cited in DN 2:10:4.

left to burn . . . when the imperfections are gone, the soul's suffering terminates, and joy remains."[8]

Although it is difficult, if not impossible, to see what is actually growing as so much seems to be being taken away, there is a new life that is being "built" within the soul, and the soul is cooperating, and actually, at some level, co-creating this new life—both through its assent to the process and through all that it does, actively and reactively, in facilitating the process. Like labor, the process of giving birth is bigger than the mother herself. It is both terribly active and terribly overwhelming, even humbling. The pains are extraordinary; the vulnerability of the mother can be frightening; and one must use a combination of strategies to give birth: "working with" birthpangs, fortifying oneself between them, availing oneself of assistance from others; and whatever battery of mental and emotional coping mechanisms one can muster. So it is with the spiritual life. Life in the Spirit is, by definition, far larger than we are. As we make spiritual progress, we will see our limitations, our "warts," our "smallness"—what John calls our "misery and poverty"—as human persons. We will consequently be invited into a largesse that we never knew we possessed. How we perceive this process will be dependent upon what we notice about it and where we put our energies and attentions. If and as we contemplate the radical changes occurring within us—transformations we come to know and see as both positive and even extraordinary, particularly as we become aware that we are changing in ways we might not have believed possible—we can appreciate that the process is, in effect, "burning" fortitude, wisdom, grace, and all the virtues and gifts that are germane to us indelibly into our being.

Ultimately what is being "birthed" in us, John tells us, is what has always been in us: God!

---

8. DN II: 10:5.

Passages from John of the Cross

The Dark Night

One dark night,
inflamed by love's urgent longings,
Oh, pure bliss!
I slipped away unnoticed,
once my home was at rest.

In darkness, yet assured
by the secret staircase, disguised,
Oh, pure bliss!
In darkness and moved by love,
once my home was at rest.

On that blessed night,
in secret, when no one saw me,
nor did I myself see anything;
and with no other light or guide
than the one burning in my heart.

That one guided me
more surely than the light of midday
to the place where waited
the one I knew so well,
in a place where no one else could come.

Oh night that guided!
Oh night more loving than the dawn!
Oh night that joined
the lover with the beloved,
beloved in the lover transformed!

Upon my flowering breast
which I preserved entirely for him;
he fell fast asleep,
and I graced him with it,
as the cedars breathed their fragrance.

The air stirred from the castle's opening,
while I caressed his hair,
and his gentle hand
was on my neck,
suspending all my senses.

I stayed and forgot myself
as I lay my face upon my Lover;
all things ceased, and I abandoned myself,
leaving all my cares
forgotten among the lilies.

Passages from John of the Cross's *Ascent of Mount Carmel*

A more enlightened knowledge and experience than mine is necessary to speak about and explain the dark night through which a soul journeys in order to arrive at the divine light of perfect union with the love of God, insofar as one can do so in this life. For the labor and darkness of the spiritual and temporal journey that souls pass through in order to arrive at this perfection are such that neither human knowledge nor experience is sufficient to be able to speak of them; only those who have gone this way will know how it feels. (AMC Prologue:1)

For that reason, in order to say something about this dark night, I will not trust either my own experience nor human knowledge, because both can fall short and deceive us. I will not fail to make use of their help when I can, but I will need above all, with God's favor—especially in what is most important and hardest to understand—to make use of holy Scripture, since we cannot fail when we use it to guide us, since the Holy Spirit speaks to us through it. And if I err in anything for not having understood well, whether or not I make use of Scripture, it is not my intention ever to separate myself from the sense and teaching of the Holy Mother Church, to whom I subject myself totally—not only to her command but also to whomever might judge more rightly. (AMC Prologue:2)

What has moved me to write this is not the capacity I see in me for such an arduous work, but the confidence that I have in God to help me to say something, because of the great need that many souls have, especially those who have begun to grow in virtue, and who then cannot move forward into union with God once Our Lord has placed them in this dark night. Sometimes they don't want to enter it or let themselves be taken into it, sometimes they don't know themselves well enough or they lack appropriate and awakened guides who can guide them along to the summit. It is a pity to see many souls to whom God gives both talent and the favor to move forward, who, if they were encouraged to take heart, would arrive at this high state. But instead they stay in a shallow way of communing with God, either because they do not want or know how to move forward or because they have no one to teach them to break away from their beginners' ways. But even when our Lord favors them so much that they can advance without this or that help, they arrive much later and with far more work and less merit than they might have, since they do not adapt themselves to collaborate with God, allowing themselves to be placed on the pure and certain road to union. For even though it is true that God is carrying them along—and can certainly carry them without these other means—they do not let themselves be carried; and in that way they advance far less, even resisting those who would help them, and they merit less because they do not apply their will to the journey, and for this reason they suffer more. Indeed there are souls who, instead of allowing God to help them, actually hinder God by their indiscreet labor and contradiction, like little children who, in wanting their mothers to carry them in their arms, go about kicking and crying, then stubbornly persisting in going on their own two feet, but not really being able to walk at all, and if they do move forward, it will be at the pace of a small child. (AMC Prologue:3)

Thus, so that people will know how to let themselves be led by God when His Majesty wants to move them forward, whether they be beginners or more advanced, I will, with God's help, give them some teaching and counsels, so that they understand better or at least let themselves be led by God. Because some spiritual directors, especially those lacking light and experience of these ways, are more likely to impede and even damage these souls than to help them on their way. . . . For this reason it is bitter and difficult in those times when a soul cannot understand itself and finds no one else who understands it, either.[9] Because it can easily happen that God draws a soul along

---

9. Cf. Teresa IC II:1:6, p. 26 above: "Oh, good Lord! Your help is so necessary here! Without it we

a sublime path of dark and obscure contemplation and dryness, and she feels herself lost, and then, being in the midst of these trials and darkness, pressures and temptations, she may find herself with someone who tells her, like Job's friends, that all of this is due to melancholy or depression or her own temperament or even that it is due to some awful sin or fault of hers, and that God has abandoned her, and then they tend to judge that this soul has lived a very bad life since such things are happening to her. (AMC Prologue:4)

Others will tell her that she should turn back, since she no longer finds satisfaction or consolation in her life with God. Such "help" only doubles the trials of the poor soul, since the worst pain she feels is the understanding of her own misery. That she is full of sins and shortcomings is clearer to her than the light of day, for God is giving her the light of understanding through that dark night of contemplation. And when she finds someone who confirms what she is feeling, telling her that all of this is her own fault, the pain and anxiety of the soul increases without end, often becoming worse than death. And not stopping there, these same confessors, judging that her struggles are due to her own sins, have such souls review their lives and put them through general confessions, crucifying them anew, not understanding that perhaps this is not the time for such a thing. Rather, they should allow them to move through whatever purgation God is working in them, and they should focus on consoling and strengthening them to bear with the process for as long as God wills, for there is no other real remedy, no matter what the soul does or the confessor says. (AMC Prologue:5)

We shall cover all of this, with God's help, and how the soul should manage and how the confessor should work with her, and what signs there are in order to recognize that this is the purgation of the soul, and, if it is, whether it is the purgation of the sense or the spirit (which is what we call the "dark night"), and how one can recognize if it is melancholy or some other imperfection of the sense or spirit. . . . All

---

cannot do anything. In Your mercy, do not let this soul be deceived and then leave off what she has begun! Give her light so that she . . . turns away from bad companions."

of this, with God's help, we will try to explain, so that all who read this might better recognize their own path and the path that is best to take in order to arrive at the summit of this mountain. (AMC Prologue:6–7)

For this reason readers should not be surprised to find the teaching about the dark night through which the soul must pass in order to reach God difficult and even a little obscure. Indeed, this will likely be the case at the outset, as they begin to read, but then it will be easier to understand better, because later stages help clarify earlier ones. Afterward, if you go back and read a second time, I think it will seem clearer and the teaching more helpful. And if some people are not helped by this teaching, it will be because of my inadequate knowledge and awkward style, because the material in itself is good and very necessary. But it seems to me that even if it were written in a polished and almost perfect way, only a few people would benefit from it, because what is written here is not so much about all the sweet and savory things about God. Rather this is a substantive and solid teaching, aimed at all who want to reach the nakedness of spirit that is elaborated here. (AMC Prologue:8)

***

Now it remains to give some counsels in order to know how to enter into this night of the senses. The first thing is to know that ordinarily the soul can enter into this night of the senses in two ways: active and passive.[10] The active way pertains to what the soul can do and does for its part in order to enter into it, and that is what we will speak of in the following counsels. The passive way consists of what the soul cannot do, because it is God who works in it and the soul takes in this work, and we will speak of this in the fourth book. (AMC I:13:1)

---

10. For commentary on these passages, see Matthew, *Impact of God*, 46–50. The terms "active" and "passive" contribute to difficulties in later interpretation of John, since they imply passivity on the soul's part, when it is probably more accurate to think of the "passive" purgation as referring to the kinds of purgation that the soul is incapable of accomplishing by itself. Even when grace is the primary (or exclusive) "actor" (*motus*) in the work, however, that does not mean that the human person is not cooperating through both his consent and disposition to be changed. Teresa favors language about "what God works in the soul; I mean the supernatural." (See, e.g. IC I:2:7 and IV:1:1).

Although the following counsels for conquering the appetites are few and short, I believe that they are as helpful and efficacious as they are concise, so that those who really want to follow them will find that they do not need any others because these contain everything. (AMC I:13:2)

And so to mortify and pacify the four natural passions, which are joy, hope, fear, and sorrow . . . , you should always incline not so much to what is easy but what is more difficult; not toward what is more pleasing but to what is more unpleasant; not toward what is more agreeable but toward what is less agreeable; not to what gives rest but to what requires more work; not to what consoles but rather to what does not console; not to what is more but to what is less; not to what is highest and most precious but to what is least and most despicable; not to wanting something but to wanting nothing; not to go about looking for the best of temporal things but the worst; and, for the sake of Christ, to desire to enter into poverty, emptiness and self-stripping with respect to all that there is in the world. (AMC I:13:5-6)

And you should embrace whole-heartedly these practices and try to overcome the will through them; for if you practice them with earnestness, you will quickly find great delight and consolation in them, practicing them with order and discretion. (AMC I:13:7)

***

And so, to understand what this union is that we are going to discuss, we should note that God dwells and is substantially present in every soul, even in that of the greatest sinner in the whole world. And this kind of [substantial] union between God and creatures is always our deepest truth, and in it we are preserved in our very being; indeed, if we were ever to lack it, we would at once be annihilated and cease to be.

So, when we speak of the union of the soul with God, we are not speaking of this substantial union that is always at work, but rather of the union and loving transformation of the soul with God, which is not always accomplished in us, but only when there is a true likeness of the two in love. This union will be called "the union of likeness," whereas the other is called essential or substantial union. That one is called "natural" and this one is supernatural, and it describes a union in which the two wills, the soul's and God's, are made into one, there being nothing in the one that conflicts with the other; so that, when the soul rids itself completely of what conflicts with or does not conform to the loving will of God, it will be completely transformed in God through love. (AMC II:5:3)

For this reason the soul must strip itself of all that is created, even its actions and abilities, including its way of understanding, of tasting and sensing, so that, free of all that is dissimilar to or not in conformity with God, it comes to receive the likeness of God, and there is nothing left in it that is contrary to the will of God, and thus it is transformed into God.[11] So that, although it is true, as we have said, that God is always present in the soul, giving and preserving its being, God does not always give it supernatural being, because this is only communicated through love and grace, and not all souls are disposed to this. And those that are, are not always disposed to the same degree, for some are greatly advanced in love and others less. And God communicates Godself more to those who have advanced farther in love—that is, to those whose wills are more conformed to the will of God, and those who are totally conformed and likened to God are united and transformed in God supernaturally. So that, from what has been said, the more that the soul is clothed in creatureliness and is subject to its own affect and habits, the less inclined it is toward this union, because it does not make total space for God to transform it supernaturally. So that the soul does not need to do anything more than strip itself of these natural contrarieties and dissimilarities, so that God, who is always communicating with us naturally in our own nature, can also communicate supernaturally through grace. (AMC II:5:4)

. . . This is what it says in John 3:5: Whoever is not reborn of the

---

11. This passage clearly demonstrates that the aim of the self-stripping is both a "nada" and a total fullness in God. See below, as well, "total space for God to transform it supernaturally" and "stripping oneself, for God, of all that is not God . . . and it possesses all that God possesses."

Holy Spirit will not see the reign of God, which is the state of perfection and rebirthing in the Holy Spirit in this life, as a soul assimilates to God in purity, without having in itself any mix of imperfection; and in that way a pure transformation is effected by participation in union, although not essentially. (AMC II:5:5)

And so that this can be understood better, let's draw an analogy: A ray of sunlight is shining through a glass window. If the window is in some way veiled by stains or cloudiness, the sunlight cannot make it clear and transform it totally in its light, in the same way that it could if it were free of those stains and clean. Indeed, the less stripped it is of those veils and stains, the less clear it can be, and the more free it is, the clearer. And this is not because of the ray but because of the glass; so that, if it were clean and pure of everything, the ray would transform and brighten it, so that it would seem to be the very same ray, and it would give off the same light as the ray, even though the glass which seems to be the same ray of light has its own nature distinct from that of the ray. But we can say that the glass is a ray or a light by participation. And so the soul is like that glass in which God is always shining—or, to say it better, the divine light of God's being dwells always in us by nature, as we have said. (AMC II:5:6)

The soul makes a place for God by removing every veil and stain of creatureliness, which consists of having our will perfectly united with that of God, because to love is to work at stripping oneself, for God, of all that is not God. Then it is left illumined and transformed in God and God communicates God's own supernatural being to it in such a way that it seems to be the same God and it possesses all that God possesses. And this union is effected when God grants this supernatural mercy to the soul, and then all things both of God and the soul are made one in a participative transformation; and the soul seems to be more God than soul, and it even is God by participation, even though it is true that its being is still naturally as distinct from that of God as before, even though it has been transformed—just as the glass remains different from the ray, even being brightened by it. (AMC II:5:7)

Passages from John of the Cross's *The Dark Night*, Book I

In this first stanza,[12] the soul speaks of the way she had of departing from self-love and the love of all things, dying by true mortification in all things including self, so that she could come to live a life of sweet and pure love with God. And she says that this departure of self and of all things was a "dark night" which here means purgative contemplation, which we will explain in a moment, but which passively causes in the soul the said negation of the self and of all things. (DN Prologue:1)

And she says that she was empowered in this departure by the strength and warmth of the love of her Spouse given to her in this obscure contemplation; and she was urged on by the pledge of love that she had as she set off to God through this night so happily. . . . And the verse says:

One dark night,

Souls begin to enter into this dark night when God draws them out of their state as beginners, which includes those who practice meditation on the spiritual road, and begins to place them in the state of proficient, or those who are already contemplatives, so that, by passing through this state, they may arrive at the state of the perfect, which is the state of divine union of the soul with God. For a better understanding and declaration of what this dark night is that the soul passes through, and why God places her in it, it will first be helpful to speak of some of the characteristics of beginners. Even though brief, this will be helpful to beginners because, understanding the weakness of their state, they will take heart and desire that God place them in this night where the soul is strengthened and fortified in virtue and advances to the inestimable delights of the love of God. . . . (DN I:1)

It should be known how God tends to the soul who has determined to devote herself to God, since God routinely nurtures it spiritually,

12. John begins his commentary on the poem "The Dark Night" above. I have translated most pronoun references to the soul as "she" rather than "it," because the poem is warmly interpersonal.

giving it many favors, just like a loving mother tends to her tender baby, warming it with the heat of her breasts, nursing it with sweetest milk and tender food so that it grows, and holding it close in her arms and caressing it lovingly. But then, as it grows older, the mother withdraws a bit, withholding so many caresses and hiding this tender love, and even putting bitter herbs on her sweet breasts, setting the child down from her arms, so that it can learn to walk, because, as it loses the characteristics of a baby, it must move onto greater and more substantial things. And the grace of God, the loving mother,[13] then regenerates and grows the soul with a new fervor and desire to serve God, since, in this stage, God lets her find sweet and delectable milk, with no effort on the soul's part in all that God gives her, and even takes great satisfaction in committing herself to her spiritual exercises, because God nurses her with tender love from the breast, just as to a tender infant.[14] (DN I:1:2)

And thus, she delights in spending long times in prayer, sometimes even entire nights, she finds satisfaction in penance, she draws content from fasting, and she takes consolations from the sacraments and from spiritual conversations. (DN I:1:3)

**

It is enough to have referred to the many imperfections that beginners have, in order to see the great need they have for God to place them into the state of proficient. God does this by putting them into this dark night, which we will now describe. It is here where God now weans them of the breasts of these gratifications and delights and, through dryness and interior darkness, God takes away all that is distracting and childish and has them gain virtues by very different means. Because even though the beginner uses his actions and passions to mortify himself in everything, he can never rid himself of everything, for as much as he tries, until God does this in him, passively, by way of the purgation of this dark night. May God grant me light, that I

---

13. See Wisd. of Sol. 16:25.
14. See 1 Pet. 2:2–3.

may say something beneficial, because in a night as dark and with such challenging material, that light is necessary. And so the verse goes:

One dark night. (DN I:7:5)

This night, which we say is contemplation, causes two kinds of darkness or purgation in spiritual persons, according to the two parts of a person—the sensory and the spiritual. And so, one night or purgation will be sensory, by which the senses are purged, and the other night or purgation is spiritual, by which the soul is purged and stripped according to the spirit, thereby preparing it and making it ready for union with God. The sensory night is common, and many pass through it, and they are beginners, of whom we shall treat first. The spiritual night is for far fewer people, those who are already tried and proficient, of whom we will treat second. (DN I:8:1)

The first purgation or night is bitter and terrible for the senses, as we shall describe; but the second is horrible and frightful to the spirit, and so, it is without comparison. And because the sensory night comes first, we will say briefly something first about the sensory night. But there is more written about it because it is more common, so we shall spend a lot longer speaking about the spiritual night, since less is spoken or written about it, and even the experience of it is rare. (DN I:8:2)

Since the conduct of beginners on the way of God is lowly and oriented to the love of self and its own satisfactions, God wants to move them forward and take them out of this lower way of loving and move them toward a higher degree of love of God, freeing them from a lower exercise of their senses and of discursive meditation, by which they search for God rather inadequately and with so many difficulties, and placing them, instead, in the full possession of their spirit, so that they can communicate with God more fully and free of their imperfections. God does this after they have followed the way of virtue, persevering in meditation and prayer, and in the delight and joy they have found there, they have lost their liking for worldly things. They have also gained spiritual strength in God (by which they have restrained their appetite for creatures), and thus, they are able to suffer with God some challenge and dryness without turning back on the way. Then, as they are going about these spiritual exercises quite happily and eagerly and when they think the light of the sun of divine favors is shining upon them, God darkens all of this light and closes the door and dries up the stream of sweet spiritual water that they enjoyed in God as often and as long as they wanted. For since they were weak and immature, there was no door closed to them, as John says in the Apocalypse (Apoc. 3:8). But now they are left in so much darkness that they do not know where to go. Their senses and imagination and discursive meditation do not move them forward even a step, in the ways that they used to (now that the interior sensory faculties are engulfed in this night), but rather, they leave them so dry that not only do they find no satisfaction or refreshment in spiritual exercises and works, but, on the contrary, they find them tasteless and even bitter. As I said, when God sees that they have grown some, God removes them from the sweet breast, so that they can grow stronger, and puts them down on the ground, so that they can begin to walk on their own two feet. And this feels like a great novelty to them, because now everything seems to be functioning backwards. (DN I:8:3)

This commonly occurs to people who are recollected, since they are freer of occasions for backsliding and they more quickly reform their appetites for worldly things—both of which are necessary in order to enter into this blessed night of sense. Ordinarily, not much time passes after they have started [the spiritual journey] before they enter into the night of the sense, and the majority of them do enter into it, because it is common to see people fall into this dryness of spirit. (DN I:8:4)

The reason for this dryness is because God moves the gifts and strength from the senses to the spirit, and because the natural senses and strength are incapable of pure spirit, they remain deprived, dry, and empty. While the spirit is tasting, the flesh tastes nothing at all and becomes weak. But the spirit, who receives this nourishment, grows strong and more alert and more solicitous than before, so as not to disappoint God. If, at first, the soul does not experience savor and spiritual delight, but rather, dryness and distaste, this is because of the novelty of the exchange. Since its palate is accustomed to these other sensory tastes (and still has its eye on them) and because the spiritual palate is not yet accustomed or purged toward such a subtle taste, until it has been gradually prepared for them by way of this dry and dark night, it cannot experience the joy and spiritual good being offered it, but rather, it feels dryness and distaste, because of the lack of that gratification it formerly enjoyed so often. (DN I:9:4)

At the time of the drynesses of this night of the sense—in which God makes the exchange that we described above, taking the soul from the life of the sense to the life of the spirit, which is from meditation to contemplation, where the soul cannot use its own faculties to work or meditate discursively on the things of God, as has been said—spiritual people can suffer real affliction, not so much because of the dryness, but because of the concern they feel that they have lost their path. They do not find support in any good thing, and so, they think their time of blessing is over and that God has abandoned them. And so, they grow weary and strive, as they are accustomed to doing, to concentrate their faculties and derive something from their discursive meditation, and they think that if they are not doing that, then they are doing nothing. And as they do this, they come into conflict with the interior of their soul, which delights in remaining in this quiet and idleness, without any operation of the faculties. Consequently, by disrupting the one process and not gaining anything by the other, they lose the space of tranquility and peace that they had. . . . But [here], it is useless for the soul to try to meditate, because it will no longer profit by that way of proceeding. (DN I:10:1)

If they cannot find someone who understands them, they turn back, leaving the path or growing weak, or at least, they do not go forward, despite the great effort they expend in trying to proceed on the way of discursive meditation, wearying and working too hard with their natural powers, imagining that they are failing because of their negligence or sins. This is understandable, because God is leading them by a different way, which is contemplation, completely different from the previous way, which is of discursive meditation, and the other way has nothing to do with our imaginative or discursive powers. (DN I:10:2)

Those who find themselves in this situation should console themselves by persevering in patience, not being afflicted. Let them trust in God, who does not leave those who search for God, with a simple and upright heart.[15] Nor will God refrain from giving them what is necessary for the journey, even bringing them to the clear and pure light of love, which God gives them by means of this other night—the dark night of the spirit—if they merit that God place them there. (DN I:10:3)

The way of proceeding that they should take in this night of sense is to leave aside discursive meditation, since it is not the proper time for that. Rather, they should leave the soul in peace and quiet, even though it clearly seems to them that they are not doing anything, and in fact, are wasting time, and, they even think that their failure to think of anything is due to some weakness on their part.[16] But they will be doing a great deal just by having patience and persevering in prayer without doing anything.[17] The only thing they really must do here is leave the soul free from all thoughts and cares, not worrying about what they will think about or meditate on, contenting themselves only with a loving and peaceful attentiveness to God. And they should be without care and without pretense of efficacy and without desire to experience or feel God, because all of these pretensions disturb and distract the soul from the peaceful quiet and sweet idleness of contemplation that is given to it here. (DN I:10:4)

Passages from John of the Cross's *The Dark Night*, Book II

This dark night is an inflow of God into the soul, which purges the soul of all ignorances and imperfections—habitual, natural, and spiritual. Contemplatives call it infused contemplation or mystical theology, in

---

15. Wisdom 1:1.
16. Cf. IC IV:1:13.
17. Cf. IC IV:1:14.

which God teaches the soul in secret and instructs us in the perfection of love, without our doing anything or understanding how this happens. This infused contemplation, since it is the loving wisdom of God, has two principal effects on the soul: it prepares the soul, purging us and illuminating us for the union of love with God. (DN II:5:1)

But a doubt arises: why, if it is a divine light (for, as we have said, it illumines and purges the soul of its ignorances), does the soul call it a dark night? There are two reasons this divine Wisdom is not only night and darkness for the soul, but also hardship and torment: the first is because of the height of the divine Wisdom, which so exceeds the soul's capacity, and so, in this way, it is darkness; the second is because of the soul's lowness and impurity, and for this reason, it is painful, afflictive, and also, dark. (DN II:5:2)

And it is clear that this dark contemplation is painful to the soul at the beginning, because, since this divine infused contemplation has many excellent properties and the soul who is receiving them is not purged and has many miseries, and because two contrary things cannot coexist in the subject of the soul, by necessity, the soul feels pain and suffers, because she is the subject in whom those two contrary things work against one another as the purgation of the imperfections of the soul is accomplished. (DN II:5:4)

Under the stress of this weight and oppression, the soul feels herself so far from favored that she thinks that even what used to provide support is now gone, along with everything else, and there is no one who will take pity on her. It is in this sense that Job, too, cried out: "Have pity on me, my friends, for the hand of God has touched me."[18] How amazing and pitiful it is that the soul is so weak and impure that, even though the hand of God is mild and sweet, the soul feels it to be heavy and contrary. For this touch of God does not weigh down the soul, but only touches her—most mercifully, at that—for God's aim is to bestow favors on the soul, not to punish her. (DN II:5:7)

Inflamed by love's urgent longings,

---

18. Job 19:21.

In this second verse, the soul describes the fire of love that we have spoken of, that, like an actual fire acts on wood, takes flame in the soul in this arduous night of contemplation. This enkindling in love . . . occurs in the spirit and, in the midst of inner darkness, she feels vividly and keenly wounded by a strong divine love and a certain feeling and foretaste of God, although the soul does not understand anything all that precisely since, as we say, the understanding remains in darkness. (DN II:11:1)

The spirit here feels itself impassioned in a great love, because this spiritual enkindling makes for a passionate love. Since this love is infused, it is more passive than active, but in this way, it engenders in the soul a strong passion of love. Already, this love carries with it something of union with God, and thus, it participates in the properties of that union, which means that the activity in it is more of God than of the soul—and thus, they take hold in the soul a bit more passively—although the soul has the role here of consenting to them. But only the love of God—which is here being united to the soul—imparts the heat, the strength, the temper and the passion of love, or enkindling, whatever the soul calls it. And the more enclosed, withdrawn, and subdued are the soul's appetites toward any particular thing, whether in heaven or on earth, the more this love will find space and disposition for uniting and adhering to it. (DN II:11:2)

This dark purgation happens in this way: God weans and recollects the soul's appetites in such a way that they cannot find satisfaction in what they want. God does this so that, in withdrawing them from other things and recollecting them in God, the soul has more strength and capacity to receive this strong union of love from God. Then, in this purgative way that God begins to give, the soul loves with great strength and all of its sensory and spiritual appetites. And this could not be if its appetites were scattered by seeking satisfaction in other things. And for this reason, so that he could receive the strength of love from union with God, David said to God: "I will keep my strength for You,"[19] which is to say: I do not want to employ the operation of all

---

19. Ps. 58:10.

of my capacity and appetites and the strength of my faculties or find satisfaction in anything but You. (DN II:11:3)

Then in some way, one might consider just how strong this enkindling of love in the spirit will be, when God gathers all of the soul's strength, faculties, and appetites, spiritual and sensory, so that the entire harmony of energy and power might be employed in this love. Thus, without disdaining anything human or excluding anything from this love, the soul can truly fulfill the first principle, which says: *You will love your God with all your heart, all your mind, all your soul, and all your strength.*[20] (DN II:11:4)

When the soul is wounded, touched, and impassioned and all of the appetites and forces of the soul are recollected here in this enkindling of love, how can we understand the movements and impulse of all of these strengths and appetites? Since they are enkindled and wounded by this strong love, and yet, still not completely in possession of it, they remain in darkness and doubt, suffering hunger like dogs that, as David says, who wander around the city and howl and sigh because they are not filled with this love.[21]

The mere touch of this divine love and fire so dries the spirit and enkindles in it the desire to satisfy its thirst for this divine love that it turns these longings over a thousand times within itself and pines for God in a thousand ways, its desire is so fierce. David explains this well in a psalm that says: "My soul thirsts for You; in how many ways does my body long for You!"[22] And another translation puts it this way: "My soul thirsts for you; my soul loses itself and dies for You." (DN II:11:5)

This is why the soul in this verse is "inflamed by love's urgent longings" and not "inflamed by love's urgent longing," because in all the thoughts that cycle round in its mind and in all of its affairs and in the things that happen to it, it loves in many ways, and it desires and even suffers in desire in many ways, and in all times and places, not really able to find rest in anything, since it feels this urgency in the burning wound, like the prophet Job says: "As the servant desires

20. Dt. 6:5
21. Ps. 58:7, 15–16.
22. Ps. 62:2.

the shade and as the hireling desires the end of his work, so I have had months of misery and long and troubled nights. And if I lie down to sleep, I say, 'When will I arise?' Then the night drags on; I am filled with restlessness until the dawn."[23]

Everything becomes narrow for this soul; it is outgrowing itself, and it does not fit in heaven or on earth, and it is filled with sorrows unto darkness, just as Job says here, speaking spiritually to our point. It is painful, and the soul endures without the consolation of hope in any light or spiritual good. So that the urgency and affliction the soul feels in this burning love is words, because it is doubly increased: first because of the spiritual darkness and the doubts and fears that afflict it, and second, because of the love of God that burns and stimulates and even marvelously stirs it with its loving wound. (DN II:11:6)

These two ways of suffering at the same time Isaiah explains clearly, saying "My soul yearns for you in the night[24]–that is, in the midst of misery. This is one way of suffering because of this dark night. "But my spirit," he says, "within me keeps vigil for you." And that is the second way of longing and urgency and the part of the love that is in the innermost parts of the spirit. Nonetheless, in the midst of these dark and loving longing, the soul feels a certain presence and a strength in its interior, that accompanies and strengthens it so much that, when the weight of this narrow darkness goes away, it feels itself alone, empty, and weak. And the reason is that when the darkness ends, so does the strength and efficacy of the soul, which is joined passively to the dark fire of love that now has a hold on it. (DN II:11:7)

John's *Spiritual Canticle*

Prefatory comment to the *Spiritual Canticle*:

John's "Spiritual Canticle" has an extraordinary compositional history. The first 31 stanzas were written on scraps of paper given to him by a sympathetic guard while he was imprisoned by his Calced brothers

23. Job 7:2-4.
24. Isa. 26:9.

in Toledo. John knew the Song of Songs by heart, and the images of love and nature contained within it must have been a balm for his immediate affliction in prison. The "Spiritual Canticle" is both a hymn to the beauty of creation, not unlike an expansive version of Francis of Assisi's famous Canticle of the Creatures, and an epic saga of the soul's passionate and tumultuous journey toward deepest union with God, patterned after the Song of Songs. The poem articulates a profound sense of the soul's longing for God and God's own captivation with the human person in such a way that the reader comprehends the force and power of love as an agent of constant dynamism and transformation. As in the Song of Songs, the dynamic energy of love is not simply a human experience. In the "Spiritual Canticle," God is not immune to love, but is its source, object and subject. Repeatedly, God is an actor in the drama of relational love, inspiring the soul's desire for union, and then, moved by the soul and its devotion and dedication to the way of love, rewarding it.

Although commentators on John of the Cross and on *The Spiritual Canticle* often focus on the soul's "surrender" to God, the actual text of the poem, like the Song of Songs itself, in many ways, cautions us against such an approach to the divine–human relationship. Over and over, the soul's/bride's steadfastness, strength and determination is noted, affirmed, and celebrated. In stanza 3, for example, she determines to go out of herself and away from her homeland, out to "the mountains and watersides," without lingering on the journey and without fear of danger or attack—single-minded in her quest for mystical union.

> Seeking my Love
> I will head for the mountains and for watersides,
> I will not gather flowers,
> nor fear wild beasts;
> I will go beyond strong men and frontiers.[25]

25. John of the Cross, "Spiritual Canticle" stanza 3; for discussion, see below, pp. 97–98. Here, the clarity of purpose represented in the soul's search for God recalls Clare of Assisi's counsel in her second letter to Agnes of Prague (1235): "With swift pace, light step, unswerving feet, so that even your steps stir up no dust, may you go forward, securely, joyfully, and swiftly, on the path of

As she makes her way toward the mountains, she calls upon all the elements of nature ("O woods and thickets,/planted by the hand of my Beloved!/O green meadow,/coated bright, with flowers,/tell me, has he passed by you?") to help her in her search, and, when she gets no response she commands:

> . . . [S]urrender yourself!
> Do not send me
> any more messengers;
> they cannot tell me what I must hear.[26]

Like the Song of Songs, the poem "Spiritual Canticle" is in dialogue form, with the majority of the stanzas spoken by the bride, or human person. For the first twelve stanzas, the bride speaks of her desire for union with her beloved, alternately addressing her beloved (who is not, as yet, physically present), herself, or her environs. This section addresses the inner qualities necessary to approach union with God, focusing most directly on the intensification of desire for union which gives the soul the perseverance, fortitude, and energy for the journey. Throughout these stanzas, the voice of the bride gathers strength and clarity until, in stanza 11, she commands,

> Reveal your presence,
> and may the vision of your beauty be my death;
> for the sickness of love
> is not cured
> except by your very presence and image.[27]

The Bridegroom responds in the thirteenth stanza with a brief intervention, which seems only to indicate his presence, and perhaps, his location. While the response affirms the soul's search, there is no clear invitation expressed to the bride; rather, the statement is an enigmatic, muted reply to the bride's entreaties:

---

prudent happiness . . ." in *Clare of Assisi: Early Documents* trans Regis J. Armstrong (New York: New City Press, 2006), 47–49 at 48.

26. John of the Cross, "Spiritual Canticle," stanza 6.

27. Ibid., 11.

Return, dove;
the wounded stag
is in sight on the hill,
cooled by the breeze of your flight.[28]

The final five stanzas of the "Spiritual Canticle" appear to have been inspired by a comment made by the prioress of Beas, Madre Francisca de la Madre de Dios. Asking her about how she prayed, she told John that her technique was simple: she beheld God's beauty and rejoiced in it. The simplicity of the answer captivated John, and the final five stanzas celebrate God's beauty.[29]

Passages from John's *Spiritual Canticle* Stanza 3

Seeking my love
I will go to the mountains and riversides;
I will not gather flowers,
nor fear wild beasts;
I will go beyond strong men and frontiers.

Now, the soul sees that neither her sighs nor her prayers nor the help of good intermediaries are enough to find her Beloved. And because the desire with which she seeks him is authentic and her love is very great, she does not leave anything on her part untried. For the soul that truly loves God is not lazy about doing everything she can to find her Beloved; even when she has tried everything, she is still not satisfied and thinks she has done but little. (SCB 3:1)

To truly find God, it is not enough to pray with the heart and the tongue, nor to avail oneself of the help of others, but also, in addition to all of that, it is necessary for her to do everything that is in her to do, because God tends to esteem the work that a person does more than the work that is done for that person. And for that reason, the soul, remembering the words of her Beloved, "Seek and you shall find,"[30] is determined to go out searching in the way we mentioned, through works, so that she is not left without finding him. . . . The bride in the

---

28. John of the Cross, "Spiritual Canticle," stanza 13.
29. Recounted in "Introduction to *The Spiritual Canticle*" in CWJC, 400.
30. Luke 11:9.

Song of Songs cried out for him, but she did not find him until she went out looking for him: "In my bed at night I sought the one who loved my soul; I sought him and did not find him; now I will get up and go around the city; in the outskirts and the squares I will look for the one who loves my soul." And then, after passing through hardships, she said she found him. (SCB 3:2)

"I will not gather flowers ..."

Since seeking God requires a heart, naked, strong, and free from all evils and goods that are not God, the soul speaks in this verse and the following ones about the freedom and fortitude one should possess in order to seek God. . . . The one who wants to advance should not linger to gather flowers, but should have the courage and strength to say "nor will I fear wild beasts; I will go beyond strong men and frontiers." (SCB 3:5)

According to David, "Many are the tribulations of the just, but the Lord will deliver them from all of them (Ps. 33:20). But the soul who is truly in love and who esteems her Beloved more than all other things, trusting in his love and kindness, finds it easy to say, "nor will I fear wild beasts, and I will go beyond strong men and frontiers." (SCB 3:8)

Such is the way the soul, in this stanza, says is the way to search for the Beloved: she must have steadfastness and courage in not leaning down to pick flowers; courage so as not to fear wild beasts; strength in passing by strong men and frontiers; and the sole intention of going toward the mountains and watersides of the virtues. (SCB 3:10)

***

The soul's strength fortifies her longing, so that, just like a stag when wounded by an arrow neither rests nor calms down, searching here and there for remedies . . . so the soul, impatient with love, will endure no idleness nor rest in its pain, showing its longings in every way until it discovers a remedy. (SCB 9:1-2)

The soul in love, however great her conformity to her Beloved, cannot stop loving . . . until it reaches the perfection of love, which is to say, with Love itself . . . The soul, then, enkindled with love of God, yearns for the fulfillment and perfection of love in order to be refreshed in it. (SCB 9:7)

***

Prefatory comment to *Spiritual Canticle* Stanza 17

By Stanza 17, the soul is beginning to enjoy "an interior union of love," which "actuates the soul in love" and in "attending to God with love," the soul begins "to love in the continuance of unitive love."[31] This experience emboldens the soul to entreat:

Spiritual Canticle Stanza 17

> Be still, deadening cold north wind;
> Come, south wind that awakens love;
> breathe through my garden
> and let your fragrances flow,
> and my Beloved will graze among the flowers.

Now, the soul does two things:

First, she impedes dryness, closing the door by way of continuous prayer and devotion. And second, she invokes the Holy Spirit, Who is the one to dispel this dryness of spirit and Who sustains and increases her love for the Spouse. The Spirit also puts into interior motion all of the virtues in the soul, with the aim that the Spouse rejoices and delights all the more in her, because, at this point, her only goal is to give joy to her Beloved. (SCB 17:2)

What she asks of the Holy Spirit is what is said in the following verse:

> breathe through my garden,

This garden is the soul. Just as she called herself above a "vineyard in flower," because the flowering virtues in her gave a sweet-tasting wine,

---

31. See *Spiritual Canticle* 16:10.

so here she calls herself a garden because the flowers of virtues and perfections that were planted within her are now coming to life and growing. (SCB 17:5)

It is significant here that the spouse does not say here "breathe in my garden," but rather, "breathe through my garden," because there is a great difference between God breathing in the soul and God breathing through the soul. To breathe in the soul is to infuse in it grace, gifts, and virtues. And to breathe through the soul is when God touches and puts in motion the virtues and perfections that have already been given to it, renewing and stirring them, so that they give off an admirable and sweet fragrance, as when aromatic spices are stirred and they spread their abundant fragrance, which, prior to this, was neither so strong nor so highly perceptible. (SCB 17:5)

In this breathing through the soul, which is the Holy Spirit's visit of love, the Spouse, who is the Son of God, sends the Spirit first (as to the apostles), Who is the host to prepare the dwelling place of the soul-bride, raising her up in delight and adorning this garden, opening its flowers, disclosing its gifts, and decorating her with a tapestry of graces and riches. . . . For this is characteristic of the Spouse: to be united with the soul amidst the fragrance of her flowers. (SCB 17:8)

The bride in the Song of Songs, as one who knows so well, describes this characteristic in these words: "My Beloved has gone down to his garden, and the air scented with aromatic spices, to graze in the gardens and gather lilies."[32] And in another place, she says: "I am for my Beloved, and my Beloved is for me, who feeds among the lilies,"[33] which is to say "My Beloved feeds and delights in my soul, which is his garden, among the lilies of my virtues and perfections and graces." (SCB 17:10)

Spiritual Canticle Stanza 20

In order to arrive at such a high state of perfection as the soul here desires, which is spiritual marriage, it is not enough to be clean and

32. Song of Songs 6:1.
33. Song of Songs 6:2.

purified of all imperfection and rebellion and imperfect habits of the inferior part in which, when the "old person" has been stripped, is now subject and yields to the superior part. It is also necessary for it to have great fortitude and a very sublime love in order to enter into the strong and intimate embrace of God. For, in this state, the soul achieves not only a radiant purity and beauty, but also, an amazing strength through the intimate and powerful bond that the union between God and the soul instills in her. (SCB 20:1)

And so the Bridgroom responds:

> Agile birds,
> lions, stags and leaping bucks,
> mountains, valleys, rivers,
> waters, winds, fires
> and vigilant fears of night;
> with charming harps
> and serene song, I order you
> to cease your storming
> and not to touch the rampart
> so that the bride can sleep securely.[34]

And in this way, the Beloved makes all of the bothersome operations and movements within the soul cease, by way of the great sweetness and delight and strength she possesses in the communication and total self-offering that God gives her in this time. And because God transforms the soul vitally[35] into God's own self, all of the powers, appetites, and movements of the soul lose their natural imperfection and are changed into divine ones. (SCB 20:4)

Being now completely fulfilled in this union with God in so far as is possible in this life, there is nothing in the world left for it to want or hope for, nor is there anything spiritual to desire, since it sees and feels itself completely full of the riches of God. . . . [T]he soul is like unto God in this respect. For, just as God takes delight in all things, God does not delight so much in them as in Godself, since God enjoys in Godself, a higher good than any other thing. And so, any new joy or delight

---

34. SCB stanzas 20–21.
35. that is, "in a living way," *vivamente*.

offered to the soul serves more as a reminder to her to delight in what she already has and feels within herself than in whatever other thing, since, as I say, who she now is [in God] is more than all these other things. (SCB 20:11–12)

And were we to want to speak of the glorious illumination which the soul is given in this habitual embrace—which is a certain turning toward her, so that she is enabled to see and enjoy together this whole abyss of delights and riches that God has placed within her—our words would fail to explain any of this. (SCB 20:14)

For in this soul, we can understand what the Wise one said: "The peaceful and tranquil soul is like a continual banquet." (Prov. 15:15) Just as in a banquet, there are flavors of every kind of food and the sweetness of all kinds of music, so the soul receives every joyful delight and all sweetness at this banquet from the breast of her Spouse. (SCB 20:15)

Prefatory comment to *Spiritual Canticle* Stanza 22

Stanza 22 of the *Spiritual Canticle* signals a transformation in the quality of the intimacy between the two lovers in the poem. Beginning with the stanza, the soul is called the "bride" or "spouse" and the "Beloved" is called the "Spouse." This signals the consummation of their union in a "spiritual marriage" that John tells us "is incomparably greater than the spiritual espousal because it is a total transformation in the Beloved, in which both parties give themselves over in a total possession one of the other, in a consummation of their union of love, and in which the soul becomes divine, becomes God by participation, in so far as this is possible in this life."[36]

Spiritual Canticle Stanza 22

The bride has entered

And thus, I think that this state does not come to pass without the soul

---

36. *SCB* 22:3.

being confirmed in grace, and such faith is confirmed in both parties, since God's faith in the soul is confirmed here as well. Accordingly, this is the highest state to which one can enter in this life, for just as in the consummation of a human marriage, the two become one flesh, as Scripture tells us (Gen. 2:24), so in the consummation of this spiritual marriage between God and the soul, two natures become one in spirit and love, as Saint Paul says, using the same manner of speaking when he says: "The one who is joined with the Lord becomes one in spirit." (1 Cor. 6:17)[37] And so, when the light of a star or a candle is joined and united with that of the sun, what shines is not the star nor the candle, but the sun, which has absorbed the other lights into its own. (SCB 22:3)

into the sweet garden she desired

This is like saying: She has been transformed into her God, who is here called "the sweet garden" because of the delightful and sweet dwelling that she now finds in God. One cannot arrive at this garden of full transformation without first passing through the spiritual espousal and the loyal and mutual love of betrothed partners. For after the soul has been the betrothed of the Son of God, in complete and sweetest love, then God calls her and places her in this flowering garden in order to consummate this most joyous estate of marriage. And the union of the two natures and the communication of the divine and the human in this state is such that, even though neither one of them changes their being, both appear to be God. Although in this life, it may not be perfectly so; still, it is beyond anything that can be said or thought. (SCB 22:5)

The very same Spouse in the Song of Songs makes this easy to see when inviting the soul (now made a spouse) into this state, saying: "*Veni in hortum meum, soror mea sponsa; messui myrrham meam cum aromatibus meis*"; which means "Come and enter my garden, my sister, my bride, for now I have gathered my myrrh with my aromatic spices."[38] He calls her "sister and spouse," because she is already those

---

37. Cf. Teresa, IC VII:2:5.
38. Song of Songs 5:1.

things in the love and self-offering she made before she was called into this state of spiritual marriage, where, as He says, He has gathered fragrant myrrh and aromatic spices, which are the fruits of the flowers now ripe and ready for the soul. These are the delights and grandeurs which, in this state, God now gives her directly of God's own self.

Consequently God is now the "sweet garden that she has desired," because all desire and every aim, of the soul and of God through all of her works, is the consummation and perfection of this state; and thus, the soul never rests until she reaches it, because she finds in this state a much greater abundance and fullness of God and a safer and more stable peace, and more perfect sweetness without compare than in the spiritual espousal. For in it, she routinely feels herself taken into an intimate spiritual embrace, which is a true embrace, through which she now lives in God. The words of St. Paul are proven in this soul when he says: "I live, now not I, but Christ lives in me."[39] (SCB 22:6)

And since the soul now lives such a glorious and felicitous life, just as God does, we should all consider, in so far as we can, what a pleasant life it is that she lives, since, just as God can never really feel troubled, neither can she, but rather, she feels joy and delight from the glory of God in the substance of her soul already transformed in God. And for that reason, the next verse continues:

> And she rests in delight,
> reclining her neck. (SCB 22:6)

The neck means, here, the strength of the soul by means of which, as we said, is effected this union between her and the Spouse, because the soul would not be able to endure so intimate an embrace if she were not already very strong. And since this strength enabled the soul to work and practice virtue and conquer vice, it is only right that in this strength in which she worked and conquered, that now she repose, reclining her neck on the gentle arms of her Beloved. (SCB 22:7)

---

39. Gal. 2:20.

Spiritual Canticle Stanza 25

> The touch of the spark,
> the spiced wine,
> all flowings of the balsam of God

This touch of the spark is a very subtle touch that the Beloved sometimes gives the soul, often when she is not expecting it, and it enkindles the heart in a fire of love, such that it seems like nothing less than a spark of fire that leaps and enflames her. And with remarkable speed, like when one suddenly remembers something, the will is enkindled in loving, desiring, praising, and thanking God, and in reverencing and esteeming and praying to God with all the savor love gives; and so, she calls all of these things the "balsam of God," which comforts and cures the soul with its fragrance and substance. (SCB 25:5)

The bride in the Song of Songs speaks of this divine touch in this way: *"Dilectus meus misit manum suam per foramen, et venter meus intremuit ad tactum eius,"* which means: "My beloved put his hand through the opening, and my heart trembled at his touch."[40] The touch of the Beloved is the touch of love which we say that God gives the soul. The hand is the favor which is granted in her at the touch. The opening through which the hand enters is the manner, mode, and degree of perfection which the soul has, because the touch can be felt in more or less of a manner, depending upon the spiritual caliber of her soul. And her heart, which here she says trembles, is the will that is touched. And the trembling is how the appetites and currents of her love of God rise up in her, pouring forth in desire, love, praise, and the other things we have said; all of these are the flowings of balsam pour forth from this touch. (SCB 25:6)

The spiced wine. This spiced wine is another, far greater favor that God sometimes gives to advanced souls in which they are inebriated in the Holy Spirit with a wine of love that is sweet and delightful and fortified. That is why it is called "spiced wine," because spiced wine

---

40. Song of Songs 5:4. The Latin "venter" here ordinarily signals the belly or uterus.

is seasoned with many and varied strong and fragrant spices, so this love, which is what God gives to those who are now perfect, has been fermented and distilled in their souls, spiced with the virtues that the soul has gained. And this wine, spiked by these precious spices, gives such force and abundance of sweet inebriation to the soul through the visits that God grants her, that they cause her to give to God, with great efficacy and force, these flowings of praise and love and reverence, along with admirable desires to work and suffer for God. (SCB 25:7)

And it should be known that this favor of sweet inebriation lasts longer than the spark, because it settles. The spark touches and then passes on, although its effect lasts for some time, and even, sometimes, quite a while. But the spiced wine—which, as I say, is the sweet love in the soul—tends to last, and its effects can remain for some time, which is to say a day or two, or even, many days, although not always with the same intensity, since it grows stronger or weaker without that being in the soul's power. In fact, sometimes without doing anything at all, the soul feels in its intimate being that its spirit is being sweetly inebriated and inflamed by this wine, according to what David says: "My heart grew heated within me, and in my meditation a fire will be enkindled."[41] Sometimes, this divine spark sets the soul on fire and leaves it burning with love. (SCB 25:8)

Spiritual Canticle Stanzas 26–28[42]

> In the interior wine cellar
> I drank of my Beloved, and when I went away,
> through all of this valley,
> I no longer knew anything,
> and lost the herd that I was following.
>
> There he gave me his breast;
> there he taught me a knowledge that I savored,
> and I gave myself to him completely,
> holding nothing back;
> there I promised to be his spouse.

---

41. Cf. Ps. 38:4.
42. Stanzas 26–28 of the *Spiritual Canticle* epitomize the consummation of union. In his commentary on these stanzas, John's explanations are permeated with references to the Song of Songs.

My soul is now totally engaged
and all my wealth in his service;
now I do not tend my herd,
nor do I have any other occupation;
now my only work is to love.

This "wine cellar" that the soul speaks of her is the final and most intimate space of love in which the soul can experience in this life; that is why it is called "the inner wine cellar," or the most intimate. And we can say that these levels or wine cellars of love are seven, and that we have them when we come to have all seven gifts of the Holy Spirit perfectly, at least in the way in which the soul is capable of receiving them. (SCB 26:3)

And it should be known that many souls arrive at and enter in the early wine cellars, each according to the perfection of love that she maintains; but very few arrive at this last and most interior one in this life, because in it, the perfect union with God that is called "spiritual marriage" has already been accomplished, of which the soul is now speaking. And what God communicates to the soul in this intimate union is completely unsayable; one cannot even say anything about it, just as one cannot say anything of who God really is. Here, this same God is the One who is communicating to the soul, and with admirable glory is transforming her into God Godself, both of them having become one. . . . And so, in order to communicate at some level what, in that wine cellar of union, she receives from God, she says nothing more (nor do I understand that she could say anything more) appropriate than what she says in the following verse. (SCB 26:4)

I drank of my Beloved

Just as a drink is diffused and flows through all of the members and veins of the body, so this communication of God diffuses itself substantially throughout the whole soul. Or, to say it better, the soul is transformed in God, according to which transformation the soul drinks of her God through her substance and through her spiritual powers. Through her understanding, she drinks in wisdom and understanding, and through her will, she drinks in the most tender love, and through the memory, she drinks in recreation and delight in the recollection and feeling of glory. That the soul receives and drinks in delight substantially, she says in the Song of Songs in this way: *Anima mea liquefacta est, ut sponsus locutus est*, which means "My soul melted as the Spouse spoke."[43] The Spouse speaking here is God's self-communication to the soul. (SCB 26:5)

And this divine drink so thoroughly divinizes the soul[44] and uplifts it and absorbs it in God that

> when I went away,
> through all this valley,
> I no longer knew anything

Because that divinization and elevation of the mind in God in which the soul remains carried away and absorbed in love, made completely into God, does not allow her to notice anything pertaining to the world. Not only does she become annihilated and estranged from all things, but also, from herself, as if she had vanished and been dissolved in love—which consists in passing out of herself and into the Beloved. And thus, the bride in the Song of Songs, after having spoken of this transformation of her love in the Beloved, refers to this not knowing in which she was left by this word: *Nescevi*, which means, "I did not know."[45] (SCB 26:14)

The soul in this space is, in a certain sense, like Adam in a state of innocence, who did not know what evil was, because she is so innocent that she does not understand evil, nor does she judge anything to be evil. And she will hear very evil things and see them with her eyes, and even then, she will not understand what they are, because she does not have the habit of evil in her, in order to judge it. For God has rid her of all imperfect habits and of the ignorance (in which she falls into the evil of sin), replacing them with the perfect habit of true wisdom; and in that way, she "no longer knows anything." (SCB 26:14)

---

43. Song of Songs 5:6.
44. Literally, "engods" it or "makes it godly"—*endiosa*.
45. Song of Songs 6:11.

Since she is truly absorbed and imbibed in that drink of love, she cannot actually be in anything else, nor can notice it . . . [and also] that transformation in God so conforms her to the simplicity and purity of God, in which there is no form or imaginative figure, that she is left clean and pure and empty of all forms and figures that she previously held, purged and radiant in pure contemplation. Just as the sun infuses its light in the window and makes it clear, and thus, erases from view all of the stains and motes that appeared on it before, but then, when the sun leaves, the smudges and stains appear as before. Even more the soul, because the effect of that act of love remains and endures in it for some time, so the not knowing also endures, so that it really cannot notice anything else until the effect of that act of love passes. And because that act of love inflamed and moved her with love, it annihilated and melted her in all that was not love, according to what we said above about David; that is: "Because my heart was inflamed, my reins were also changed, and I was brought to nothing, and I did not know."[46] The change of the reins because of this inflammation of the heart is a change in the soul into God, in all of her appetites and operations, in a new way of life, undone and annihilated in all of the old things she did before. For this reason, the prophet says that he was brought to nothing and that he knew nothing, which are the two effects that we said that this drinking in the wine cellar of God cause in us. Because not only is all of her former knowing annihilated, all of it seeming nothing to her, but also, all of her old life and imperfections are annihilated, and she is made a new person.[47] (SCB 26:17)

Spiritual Canticle Stanza 38:

There you will show me
what my soul has been seeking

The soul's entire search is aimed toward a love equal to God's. She always desired this equality both in her own nature and by grace,

46. Ps. 72:21–22.
47. Cf. Col. 3:10.

because a true lover can never be satisfied if he feels he does not love as much as he is loved. And when the soul sees that even her transformation in God and the immense love she feels there in this life still does not bring her to equal the perfection of love with which God loves her, she desires the clear transformation in glory which will bring her to equal this love. For even though she is in such a high degree of love and there is a true union of wills here, still she cannot attain the purity and power of love which she will possess in the union of glory, just as St. Paul says, "then the soul will know as she is known by God."[48] And so, therefore, she will love as she is loved by God, since then, her understanding will be God's understanding, her will will be God's will, and so, her love will be God's love. For the will of the soul is not so much lost, but united so strongly with the strength of God's will, with which she herself is loved. And this strengthens her to love God as strongly and perfectly as she is loved by God, the two wills now being united in only one will and only one godly love. This strength is that of the Holy Spirit, in Whom the soul is transformed; and in this transformation, the Spirit is truly given to the soul as the strength of this same love, supplying and augmenting what is lacking in her through this transformation in glory. And thus, in the perfect transformation of this state of spiritual marriage, which the soul reaches in this life, she superabounds in grace, and so, can love in some way through the Holy Spirit who is given to her[49] in this transformation. (SCB 38:3)

What is truly worthy of noting here is that the soul does not say that God will *give* her God's love—even though it is true that God gives it to her—but rather, that God will *show* her how to love with the perfection that she desires. So that there, not only does God give her God's love, but God also shows her how to love God as God loves her. And, in addition to showing her how to love, purely and freely without any self-interest, just as God does, God gives her to love with the same strength that God Godself loves. And so, she loves God the way God

---

48. Cf. 1 Cor. 13:12.
49. Cf. Rom. 5:5.

loves and is transformed in God's love, as we have said. It is like placing an instrument in her hands and telling her how to use it by using it jointly with her. And until reaching this point, the soul is not satisfied, nor even could she be in the next life, if she felt that she did not love God with the same totality with which God loves her. (SCB 38:4)

Spiritual Canticle Stanza 39

> The breath of the air,
> the song of the sweet nightingale,
> the grove and its pure grace[50]
> in the serene night,
> with its flame that consumes without pain

In this song, the soul declares the "what" that the Beloved gives her in this beatific transformation, declaring it in five ways: the first, which is the breath or "spiration" of the Holy Spirit of God in her and from her to God;[51] the second, which is pure jubilation in the fruition of God; the third, which is the appreciative knowledge of creatures and the magnificent array of them[52]; the fourth, which is pure and clear contemplation of the divine essence; and the fifth, which is total transformation in the immense love of God. For this reason, the verse says (SCB 39:2):

The breathing of the air

This *breathing of air* is the capacity that the soul says that God will give her there in the communication of the Holy Spirit, who, by breathing elevates the soul sublimely to its own divine breath, teaching and

---

50. Literally, "donaire," a kind of absolute perfection of a thing in itself. Kavanaugh and Rodríguez render this "its living beauty."

51. Note, in other words, that the first gift of this unitive space is the *shared breath* between us and God, like that which unites the three persons of the Trinity. This suggestion that, in mystical union, we are brought, by participation, into the life of the Trinity is precisely what Teresa suggests in the seventh dwelling places. See IC VII:1:6–7 and VII:2:6 and see discussion in *Entering*, 113–19.

52. John's inclusion of this graced appreciation of all creation is suggestive of the same impulse in St. Francis, toward the end of his life, as he writes the "Canticle of the Creatures," his hymn in praise of creation that has now become the basis for Pope Francis' recent encyclical, *Laudato Si': On Care for Our Common Home.*

making her capable of breathing in God, with the same breath of love that God the Creator breathes in Christ and Christ in the Creator, which is the Holy Spirit and which now breathes out to her, in God and Christ, through this transformation, in order to unite her in God. There would not be a true and total transformation if the soul were not transformed in the three Persons of the Most Holy Trinity in an open and manifest degree. (SCB 39:3)

And this breath of the Holy Spirit in the soul with which God transforms her into Godself gives her such sublime and delicate and profound delight that a mortal tongue cannot describe it, nor can the human understanding grasp it in any way. Because even what takes place in the communication of this temporal transformation is unspeakable, because the soul that is united and transformed in God breathes in God, and thus, breathes out to God, in Whom she is transformed, the same breath that God breathes out to her. . . . (SCB 39:3)

And we should not think it impossible that the soul be capable of such a thing as breathing in God as God breathes in her by way of participation, because, given that God grants her the favor of uniting her in the Most Holy Trinity, in which the soul is made deiform and God through participation, how can it be incredible that she also understand, know, and love in the Trinity, together with the Trinity (or, rather, that this too can be done in her) by way of communication and participation, since God works that in her, as well? This is transformation in the three Persons in power and wisdom and love, and in this way, the soul's likeness to God is known, and she was created in God's image and likeness so that she could arrive at such a resemblance.[53] (SCB 39:4)

Oh souls created for these grandeurs and invited into them, what are you doing? Why are you delaying? Your goals are too small and your own possessions impoverished! Oh sad blindness of the eyes of your soul, since you are blind to all of this light and deaf to the great calling if you do not see that in so far as you [on your own] seek greatness and

53. Gen. 1:26.

glories, you will remain low and impoverished, since you are ignorant and unworthy of these blessings. [That is why] it follows that the soul continues with the second gift of the "what" [that is given], which is. (SCB 39:7)

The song of the sweet nightingale

What is born in the soul from the breath of the air is the sweet voice of her Beloved in her, which she uses to tell him of her delightful jubilation; and thus, both of them call this "the song of the nightingale." Just as the song of the nightingale breaks forth in the springtime, once the cold and rains and transitions of winter have passed, and she provides a melody for the ear and refreshment for the spirit, so in this same communication and transformation of love that the spouse has attained in this life, now she is free and protected from all temporal disturbances and instabilities, and divested and purged of all imperfections, hardships and clouds in the sense and the spirit. So, she feels a new springtime of ease and fullness and spiritual joy, in the midst of which she hears the sweet voice of her Spouse, which is the "sweet nightingale." And that voice renews and refreshes the substance of her soul, and with a sweet and mellow voice, he calls to her, as to a soul who is now completely ready to step into eternal life, and she hears his precious voice saying: "Arise, my beloved, my beautiful one, and come! For see, the winter is past, the rains are over and gone. The flowers appear on the earth, the time of pruning the vines has come, and the song of the dove is heard in our land."[54] (SCB 39:8)

And in this voice of the Spouse, which speaks to her in the interior of her soul, the spouse feels the end of all evil and the beginning of all good. In the refreshment and protection and delightful sentiment, she, too, like the sweet nightingale, sings a new and jubilant song to God, together with God Who moves her to do this. This is why He gives her His very own voice, so that she might give hers along with His, and Together, they sing to God. For this is the aim and desire the Spouse

54. Song of Songs 2:10–12.

has: that the soul would lift up her spiritual voice in great jubilation to God, just as the very same Spouse asks of her in the Song of Songs: "Arise, my beloved, my beautiful one, and come! O my dove in the clefts of the rock, in the secret recesses of the cliff: show me your face, and let your voice resound in my ears."[55] The ears of God signify here the desires that God has that the soul give her voice over to this perfect song of joy. And so that this voice might be perfect, the Spouse asks her to sing and let her voice sound "in the clefts of the rock"—that is, in the transformation that we spoke of in the mysteries of Christ. Since, in this union, the soul rejoices and praises God with that same God, as we said about how she loves—all is done now with God, it is perfect praise and very pleasing to God. The soul is now in such perfection that her works are perfect, and thus, this voice of jubilation is sweet to God and sweet to the soul. For that reason, the Spouse said: "Your voice is sweet"[56]—not just to you but to Me as well, since through union with Me you sing to Me and with Me, like the sweet nightingale. . . . (SCB 39:9)

With a flame that consumes without pain

By "flame," here is understood the love of the Holy Spirit. And "consume," here, means to consummate and bring to perfection. The soul, in naming all of these things that the Beloved gives her and that she possesses with consummate and perfect love, is absorbed in all of them and in a perfect love that is "without pain." She says this in order to express the perfection of this love which, has these two properties, which it must have in order to be perfect: it consumes and transforms the soul in God, and the enflaming and transforming that this flame works in the soul produces no pain in the soul. And this cannot be except in the state of blessedness, where this flame is gentle love. And the transformation of the soul into it [the flame] brings a conformity and blessed satisfaction to both parts, and for that reason, it gives no pain, as it did before the soul arrived at this capacity for perfect love.

---

55. Song of Songs 2:13–14.
56. Song of Songs 2:14.

But now that it has arrived at this state, the soul rests in such sweet and conforming love with God, that being God, is, as Moses says, "a consuming fire,"[57] and thus, it does nothing more than consume and refine. (SCB 39:14)

The Living Flame of Love

Prefatory Comments to John's Living Flame of Love

If *The Spiritual Canticle* left off at the point where the soul could rejoice with her beloved in the garden of her own soul—now an expansive space of flowering plants and blossoming vines—the *Living Flame of Love* celebrates the lived partnership with God that previous cultivation has made possible. The poem is, in comparison, remarkably short, and it is spoken by the soul "in intimate union with God." The song is a celebration of the intense "swelling of the heart" that *is* our spiritual "work" with God. Once we have reached this stage of adulthood in our relationship with God, our true work, the focus of our spiritual praxis, is nothing more or less than nurturing, cultivating, manifesting, and radiating this love, this glowing, vital essential tenderness that *is* us, that has become the deepest reality of our being, even as it is a tenderness that has been implanted in us by God and fed, little by little, in what we call our journey of spiritual growth. Encounters and unitive experiences with God have given this tenderness a kind of substance in our being.[58] The transformation of our being-in-God is most easily characterized by the feeling of tenderness, but, like love, the tenderness goes beyond a mere feeling. If love is a reality, a choice, an act, a way of being, so is the tenderness that marks us in this stage. Further, this tenderness has enough "substance" in our lives that we can sustain it as a response to life circumstances and as a chosen way of being. We allow tenderness to be ours, even as we embrace

---

57. Cf. Deut. 4:24.
58. Recalling Julian of Norwich's use of the term "substantial union" to invoke an ontological sense of union that is not particularly material in nature, but that speaks to the deepest part of our being.

tenderness as a way of interacting—with ourselves, with others and with our world.

This tenderness allows the soul to stand with God as two partners contemplating the world around them and the slice of existence that the soul can offer God and begin to dream together about what their partnership can effect in the world. We can look out upon what remains of our life and begin to imagine, with God, what might want to take shape in it, given the uniqueness of our gifts and our location in a nexus of human relationships that will support us in such work. This process of imagining, in and with God, happens almost in the same way that we think of the best human partnerships co-creating in their shared lives a future in which their love bears fruit (whether in a family or in shared projects or in shared work or in a home or in any other manifestation of love). Thus, we now reach a moment in which we say, with the same humility and self-offering of the prophets Isaiah or Jeremiah: "Here I am! What shall we do?"

If the soul at the end of *The Spiritual Canticle* could cry out to God, her beloved, "Let us go . . .," she recognizes, in *The Living Flame of Love*, that the garden of herself is already beginning to blossom. And so, she asks now, "Come, my love, and let us go to see what is flowering . . . what wants to blossom . . . what wants to emerge . . . what wants to take form and shape in and through and all around us." And so, John tells us, in the prologue to his work, that there is even more to love than the intense love that we knew at the end of the *Spiritual Canticle* at the cusp of the consummation of our love in and with God. At the stage of *The Living Flame of Love* we actually live, in a sustained way, in "the highest degree of perfection one can reach in this life (transformation in God) [and thus] these stanzas treat of a love deeper in quality and more perfect within this very state of transformation."[59] It would seem that there is no form of life beyond that . . . no degree of being higher than being transformed in God. What could be more perfect than partnership with God? Nothing, of course. Except that our love can become deeper still. We "cannot pass beyond this state of

59. LF Prologue, 3.

116

transformation," yet, John assures us, "with time and practice, love can grow deeper in quality . . . and become more ardent."[60]

As it grows in quality and ardor, this love has an intimate and delicate sweetness and produces notable effects. At some basic level, the most notable of these effects is the "living flame of love" that the soul now sustains within itself. The love of God has been so poured out within us that it extends to every pore and fissure of our being. This outpouring of love is replicated in the outpouring of exclamations in John's poem itself—words of love that flow like honey or streams of water. Indeed, John says, at the beginning of his commentary, that the soul here is "bathed in glory and love . . . in the intimate part of its substance it is flooded with no less than rivers of glory, abounding in delights, and from its depths flow rivers of living water."[61] Further, John tells us that the soul is actually "singularly close to beatitude—so close that only a thin veil separates it." And if there is any yearning left within her—any part of her that has not yet entered into a state of consummation—it is the desire that this last veil of separation be torn away. For John, this veil is "the veil of this mortal life," and perhaps by this, he means all that falls short of our capacity to participate, through love, in eternity. For the soul now lives and participates in the reality of an eternal love.

The soul here has a keen sense of anything within it that is not yet completely attuned to God's goodnes. Here we want such deep and absolute resonance with all that we have experienced that we can bear no subtlety of distinction between us and God. The flame of love within bathes us in glory and refreshes us with the quality of divine life.[62] Each movement of the flame—which, John explains, is a movement of the Holy Spirit within us—communicates the glory of God, but does so incompletely, it seems, because the soul touches eternal glory through the Holy Spirit within itself, not through itself alone.[63] While this may

60. LF Prologue: 3.
61. LF I: 1. Cf. John 7:38.
62. LF 1: 3.
63. LF 1:6: "But the delight that the flaring of the Holy Spirit generates in the soul is so sublime that it makes it know that which savors of eternal life. Thus it refers to this flame as living, not because the flame is not always living but because of this effect; it makes the soul live in God spiritually

seem entirely too subtle a distinction, it might be likened to the tuning of two strings of an instrument to the same note. When the pitch of the one is so close to the other as to be off by a micro-interval, the pain of inexactitude hurts the ear and demands resolution. Given the soul's exquisite sensitivity at this stage in its development, it cannot help but feel the difference between itself and God as the impetus for "intense desire"[64] that the transformative process be entirely perfected.

The movements of God within the soul constitute "the arts and games of love," a feast of love which the soul experiences as "tender flares of delicate love" in the most intimate center of the soul. That intimate center is a "secure, substantial and delightful place" in which the two cannot be disturbed.[65] In fact, John tells us, flat out, that "the soul's deepest center is God." And this is the reality behind the vague sense of irresolution the soul still feels: because its center is God and because God is infinite, the soul can always go more deeply into God, and it always senses this. However, because this space has been deeply purified by numerous previous encounters with God, the soul has cultivated a very deep, perhaps even "perfect" sensitivity to God's presence, and this facilitates the continuing deepening of its capacity to love and "contain" God, as John writes: "the greater the purity, the more abundantly, frequently, and generously God communicates Godself." Further, "the more degrees of love it [the soul] has, the more deeply it enters into God and centers itself in God."[66] Thus, the work of transformation has, in fact, been accomplished in the soul; now, its "work" consists only in an intensification of the actuation of love in it, around and through it. John is very clear about the exalted nature of

---

and experience the life of God in the manner David mentions: *My heart and my flesh rejoiced in the living God* [Ps. 84:2]. David did not refer to God as living because of a necessity to do so, for God is always living, but in order to manifest that the spirit and the senses, transformed in God, enjoy God in a living way, which is to taste the living God—that is, God's life, eternal life. Nor did David call him the living God other than because he enjoyed him in a living way, although not perfectly, but as though by a glimpse of eternal life."

64. LF 1: 2.

65. LF 1:9. "This feast takes place in the substance of the soul where neither the center of the senses nor the devil can reach. Therefore, the more interior it is, the more secure, substantial, and delightful, because the more interior it is, the purer it is." Cf. Teresa IC VII:2:6: "The soul does not move from that center nor is its peace lost . . ."

66. LF 1:13.

this way of being. In it, the soul "can perhaps possess in this life a habit of love as perfect as in the next" and "the operation and fruition of love increase to such a degree in this state that there is a great resemblance to the beatific state."[67]

A more technical theological explanation of this process of "actuating love" within the soul would incorporate the operation of the Trinity. At this point, the Trinity dwells within the soul, "inhabiting it" such that the soul is illumined with the wisdom of Christ, delights with the Holy Spirit joined to its will, and is absorbed in the very embrace of God. John explains that this indwelling presence and activity of God within the soul is clearly a stage beyond "communication and transformation in love." While the latter make us glow like living "embers," the movement of God within us is a living fire that can shoot forth flame at any moment. Thus, John suggests, there are two forms of union: union of "love alone" and "union with an inflaming of love;" the second, an expansion of the first, provides us with a vision of peace that is glorious and tender and communicates to us every good.[68]

Part of the imperfection or lack that the soul feels has less to do with ourselves and more to do with the ongoing reality of suffering and evil in the world around us. The soul sees, knows, and experiences the self-diffusive love of God both in God and in itself. In fact, the consummation of love it has already enjoyed is diffusing out into the world, but there is a tremendous amount that still holds back the consummation of the reign of God on earth. The soul feels and laments that all creation does not share in what it has come to experience in and with God; thus, John writes, "its sigh is as great as what it lacks for the perfect possession of the adoption of the children of God. . . . However intimate may be a person's union with God, there will never be satisfaction and rest until God's glory appears, especially since the savor and sweetness of that glory is now experienced."[69] Thus, we cry out, "Now consummate! If it be your will!"

67. LF 1:14.
68. LF 1:16–17.
69. LF 1: 27; cf. Ps. 17:15.

But the soul already lives so deeply in the love of God that this cry is not one of "affliction," but of "gentle and delightful desire." Lovingly, it sets about its own work, in and with God, to contribute to the bringing about of God's reign in whatever ways it can. Like a loving gardener, tending carefully to the nurturance of flowers and blossoms and fruits, we continue in the task of cultivating love in ourselves and others and the world around us. There is a deep serenity to the soul, which cannot be taken away from it. The serenity is rooted in the union that has already been accomplished in it. Thus, it dwells, always, in the midst of the garden of the Song of Songs, in and with God, and it possesses riches. Indeed, John writes that the soul is "pure, rich, full of virtues," and even knowingly "prepared for the kingdom [to come]." Although, at one level, it lives in anticipation of that kingdom, it is already living in that kingdom at many levels of its being.[70] Insulated now by its essential union with God, this "infinite longing" in the soul produces no pain or "wound," but only a growing fullness, for the intensity of the longing is met by movements in which God "penetrates and deifies the substance of the soul, absorbing it above all being into God's own being."[71]

Passages from John's *Living Flame of Love*

The soul being so close to God that it is transformed into a flame of love, in which all three persons of the Trinity communicate themselves to it,[72] how can it be thought unbelievable that it would enjoy a trace of eternal life? Even though it cannot do so perfectly, for it does not have that condition in this life. But so exalted is the delight which the Holy Spirit flares up in it that it does know what eternal life tastes like. That is why the flame is called a living flame—not because the flame is not always living, but because it has this effect on it: it makes the soul live in God spiritually, and therefore, experience the life of God, the way David says: "My heart and flesh rejoiced in the living God."[73] (LF 1:6)

---

70. See John's discussion of consummation as the coming of the kingdom of God and the essence of the Lord's prayer in LF 1:28.
71. LF 1:35.
72. cf. Teresa, IC VII:1:6.

How tenderly you wound

That is, how tenderly you touch me with your ardor. For in so far as this flame is the flame of divine life, it wounds the soul with the tenderness of the life of God, and it wounds and stirs it so deeply that it dissolves the soul in love, so that what happened to the bride in the Song of Songs is fulfilled in the soul: she was so touched that she melted, and so, she says: "I melted when he spoke."[74] For when God speaks, this is the effect on the soul. (LF 1:7)

It is an amazing thing that love is never idle,[75] but is in constant movement, like a blazing fire emits flames everywhere, and, since its work is to wound to cause love and delight, and it is present in the soul like a living flame, it sends out wounds like most tender flares of delicate love. (LF 1:8)

And it is another amazing thing, worthy of relating, that even though this fire of God consumes so vehemently that it could consume a thousand worlds more easily than fire here on earth could burn a piece of straw, it neither consumes nor destroys the soul in which it burns. Even less does it burden it, but rather, according to the strength of its love, it divinizes and delights it, burning gently. (LF 2:3)

In the first place, it should be known that if a person is seeking God, far more is her Lover seeking her. If she sends out to God her loving desires, which, to God, are as fragrant as *the column of smoke rising laden with the perfume of myrrh and frankincense*[76], God sends out to her *the spreading perfume of with which she is attracted and runs eagerly to Him*[77], which are divine inspirations and tender caresses. And because these caresses are from God, they are encircled with a movement toward keeping perfectly the law of God and of the faith, and because of this, the soul is always being drawn closer to God. And thus, we should understand that the very desire of God, shown to us in all of the favors that God shows us through these ointments and fragrant anointings,

---

73. Ps. 83:3.
74. Song of Songs 5:4.
75. Cf. Teresa, IC V:4:10 and VII:4:14.
76. Reference to Song of Songs 3:6.
77. Reference to Song of Songs 1:3.

prepares us for even more precious and delicate anointings, given to us in the very temple of God, until the soul enters into the most tender and pure disposition worthy of union with God and substantial transformation of all of its faculties. (LF 3:28)

The soul should observe, then, that in this matter, God is the principal agent, and is like a blind person's guide, leading it by the hand to places where she would not know how to arrive, which are supernatural things that neither our understanding or our will or our memory can completely understand. And so, our principle concern should be not to place any obstacle in the way of our guide on the road that God has prepared for us, according to the perfection of God's laws and of the faith, as we have said. And this obstacle can come upon us if we allow ourselves to be guided by another blind person[78]. There are three blind people who can pull us off the path: the spiritual director, the Adversary, and ourselves. And so that the soul understands better how this can be, we will speak a little about each of the ways it can be misled. (LF 3:29)

With respect to the first, it is terribly important that the soul who wants to move forward in recollection and perfection take great care in whose hands it puts itself, because the student can become no more than the teacher, just like the child from a parent. And be aware that, with respect to this way, at least in the more advanced stages (and even the intermediate ones), it is very difficult to find an accomplished guide able to address all of the issues necessary, since, in addition to being wise and discreet, the guide must be experienced. Although the foundation for guiding the spirit is wisdom and discretion, if there is no experience of what pure and true Spirit truly is, he [i.e. the guide] will not be able to walk with the soul as God leads it, nor will he even be able to understand the way. (LF 3:30)

In this way, many spiritual directors have greatly harmed many souls, because, in not understanding the ways and properties of the Spirit, they commonly make souls lose the unction of these delicate anointings with which the Holy Spirit prepares the soul, instructing

---

78. cf. Matt. 15:14.

it instead in coarse and base ways, which they have tried or read about, but that can only serve beginners. And, because they know no more than these—and please God, they might know even some of the most basic things!—they don't want to let souls move past the very beginning steps, like discursive and imaginary ways, even though God wants to carry them forward. And thus, they try to keep them from moving beyond their natural capacity, in which a soul can make very little progress. (LF 3:31)

And so that we can understand the condition of beginners, we should note that the practice of beginners is to meditate and to do discursive exercises using the imagination. In this state, the soul needs to be given material on which to meditate and reflect. And on his own, he can do interior acts and profit from spiritual things, because, by whetting the appetite for spiritual things, he is rid of the appetite for sensual things and disaffected from worldly things. And, as the appetite is fed and even becomes accustomed to spiritual things, which bring a certain strength and constancy, then God begins to wean the soul, as they say, and place it in a state of contemplation. And God sometimes works rather quickly this way in some people, especially in vowed religious, since they have already let go of worldly things, and they accustom their senses and appetites to the Spirit as quickly as God works in them. And this happens as they let go of discursive activity and the kinds of meditation that the soul can accomplish (as well as its early sensitivities), since it is no longer able to use discursive meditation the way it did before or to find anything helpful from its own senses.... (LF 3:32)

Therefore, the person in this stage must be guided in a way that is totally opposite from her earlier way; if before, she was given material for meditation, and she meditated, now such matter must be taken away, and the person should not meditate, since she will not be able to, even if she should want to, and, were she to try, instead of recollecting herself, she would be distracted.... For now, she enjoys the peace and quiet secretly being given to her by the Spirit. That is why in this state, a director should never impose meditation or some outward act or any movement toward feeling or satisfaction, because this would place an obstacle in the way of the primary actor, who, as I have said, is God, and who is secretly and quietly at work, giving the soul wisdom and loving knowledge directly and without any specific activity (although sometimes, the soul will feel something specific for some time); and thus, the soul also should open itself completely to the loving attention of God, without doing anything in particular, but rather, holding herself completely open (or, as we have said, passively) and without doing anything on her own, but rather, with her entire loving attention directed to God. The aim is a simple and pure loving awareness, like a person who opens her eyes with loving attention. (LF 3:33)

Since here, God is communing with her through a simple and loving awareness, the soul also communes with God by receiving God with simple and loving attention, so that they are united, in attentiveness and love. For the one who receives should receive in the way that a thing is given, so that she can hold and receive what is being given. Thus, as the philosophers say, whatever thing is received is in the recipient in the same way that the recipient receives it. In this way, it is clear that if the soul does not leave behind her natural way of acting, she will only receive the good in a natural way and not in a supernatural way—therefore, she will not receive it at all, because the supernatural does not fit into the natural, nor does it have anything to do with it . . . (LF 3:34)

And for this reason, when the soul is placed in silence in this way and begins to listen, she should forget even the practice of loving awareness that I mentioned before, so that she is completely free for whatever God wants. For that loving awareness is used as a practice only when a person does not feel herself placed [by God] in this solitude (with an inner idleness) or forgetfulness or spiritual listening. And so that this can be recognized, this "being placed" comes to pass with a particular peaceful serenity and interior absorption. (LF 3:35)

Wipe away, then, oh spiritual soul, the dust and hairs and fog, and cleanse your eye! The sun will illuminate your eye, and you will see clearly! Put your soul at peace, drawing it out and freeing it from the yoke and servitude of the feeble operation of its own capacities, which is like slavery in Egypt, where everything is little more than gathering straw to make bricks.[79] And guide her, oh spiritual director, to the promised land of milk and honey. And see that this God calls the freedom and holy idleness that children of God are called to a "desert," and the soul journeys there festively clothed and with gold and silver jewelry, having now left Egypt and its riches—which is the sensory part of the person. And not only this, but the Egyptians are drowned in the sea of contemplation, where the Egyptian of the sense, not finding a foothold or anything to hold onto, drowns, and thereby frees the child of God, which is the spirit that has now emerged from the narrow limits and slavery of the operation of the senses, which means its limited understanding, its mean sensibilities, its poor way of loving and finding satisfaction, so that now, God can give it sweetest manna. . . . And so, when the soul arrives at this state, do not disturb her with concerns or requests, giving her the greatest solitude and reclusion possible, since the greater her solitude and the more closely she arrives at this idle and complete tranquility, the more abundantly the Spirit of divine wisdom can flood through her being. And this Spirit is loving, tranquil, solitary, peaceful, sweet, and totally intoxicating, such that the soul feels herself tenderly and sweetly wounded and overcome, without knowing by whom or where or how. And all of this is communicated without any operation of her own. (LF 3:38)

Whatever God works in the soul in this holy idleness and solitude, however small, is an unimaginable gift, often even more than the soul or the spiritual director can know; and even if this is not obvious immediately, its fruits will shine forth in their own time. The only clear thing that the soul can feel is a strong desire for reclusion[80] and an estrangement toward all things, sometimes more strongly than others, and she is inclined to solitude, and finds all worldly things tedious in light of the Spirit's sweet breath of love and life. (LF 3:39)

How gently and lovingly

---

79. See Exod. 1:14.
80. Even an "alienation"—enajenación.

You awaken in my breast,
where You alone secretly dwell,
and in Your sweet breath,
full of goodness and glory,
how tenderly You fill me with love.

It should be known that God dwells secretly in all souls, hidden in their very substance, for, if this were not so, they would not perdure. But there is a difference between this way of dwelling and other ways . . .[81] And it is in this soul which is now emptied of any appetite or other images or forms or affections for any created thing that this Lover dwells secretly, with an embrace so much closer, more intimate and interior, the purer and more alone the soul is to everything other than God. God's dwelling is *secret*, then, because the devil cannot enter into this embrace, nor can human understanding know what this is. But God's dwelling is not secret to the soul who abides in this perfection, for such a soul feels this intimate embrace deep within herself, although not always in these awakened ways. For when the Lover awakens her, it seems to the soul that God Godself is awakening in her, whereas before, it was as if God was asleep. So that, even though she felt and enjoyed God's presence in her breast, it was as if a loved one were present but asleep; for when one is asleep, understanding and love are not communicated to one another in the same way as when both are awakened to one another. (LF 4:14)

Oh, how happy is the soul who always feels God resting and reposing in her breast! And how appropriate for her to separate herself from everything, flee from ordinary affairs and live in immense tranquility, so that it might never disturb or trouble the breast in which the lover rests! God is there, ordinarily, as if asleep in this embrace with the spouse, in the substance of her soul, and she ordinarily feels and enjoys this presence. If she were always aware of this awakened presence, communicating love and knowledge, she would already be in glory. . . . (LF 4:15)

And when this perfect soul does feel this awakening of the Spouse

---

81. Cf. IC I:1:5.

within her, everything that is done and that occurs is perfect, because God Godself does everything, just as when someone awakens and breathes: now, the soul feels a new delight in the Breath of the Spirit of God, in which she is glorified and enamored fully. And for that reason, the following verses say (LF 4:16)

> And in Your sweet breath,
> full of goodness and glory,
> how tenderly You fill me with love.

I would not wish to speak of that breath that is so full of goodness and glory and the delicate love of God for the soul, for I see that I have no way of knowing how, and it would seem so if I did speak. For it is a Breath that God makes in the soul, in which by that awakening of sublime knowledge of the Godhead, the Holy Spirit breathes in her in the same proportion the intelligence and knowledge of God, so that she is deeply absorbed in the Holy Spirit, Who then rouses in her a love of such excellence and divine tenderness, just like the one she saw in God. For since that Breath is full of goodness and glory, the Holy Spirit filled the soul with goodness and glory, and she is enkindled in God's own love, incomprehensibly and indescribably in the depths of God, to Whom be all honor and glory forever. Amen. (LF 4:17)

4

Locating Teresa and John in the Larger Christian Mystical Tradition: A Complicated Reception

Teresa and John's writings fit into a much larger reform, of the monastic tradition and the Catholic Church at large, even as they speak to a wider Christian tradition than they themselves would probably have been able to imagine. In order to see and assess their impact and to "map" their place within that larger Christian tradition, I shall review three aspects of their reception history: (1) the initial (and somewhat mixed) response of the Christian tradition from the time of their writings until the condemnation of quietism in the late seventeenth century; (2) Teresa and John's ongoing influence as spiritual figures through the twentieth century; and (3) resurgence of interest in them in the mid-twentieth century and the ongoing integration and re-appropriation of their theological-spiritual vision, especially as it provides practical wisdom to contemporary challenges. Each of these subjects constitutes a book's worth of materials, and all I can hope to do here is to provide as comprehensive an initial summary of the issues as possible and send readers to reliable sources for further investigation.

Initial Response (c.1570–c.1700)

Teresa and John's vigorous defense of mental prayer, their united critique of the shortcomings of contemporary spiritual directors, their clarity about God's desire for deeper communion with humanity, and their constant affirmation of that possibility despite our fallen reality constituted a potent recipe for transformation. As they consciously and deliberately joined forces in Avila in 1571, each of them settled more deeply into their conscious apprehension of the mystical life, and the energy of a true reform movement, as hearts took fire, had begun. Their successful collaboration bore immediate fruit in an explosion of reforming activity: Teresa personally founded or oversaw the foundation of 17 discalced Carmelite convents and monasteries between 1565 and her death in 1582, and, as we shall see, they continued to spread throughout Europe and the Americas in the seventeenth century. But the success of the Discalced reform also generated controversy, resistance, and opposition, during their lives and after. It is this mixed immediate reaction that we will explore first, and we will begin, as it did, before they died.

In previous writing, I have suggested that Teresa's religious vocation had two complementary facets, reformer and writer; that her work as a writer of reflections on the mystical life was an integral part of her reform; and that her endeavors in both arenas awakened significant resistance even as they contributed substantively to the Catholic Reformation.[1] That statement is true of both Teresa and John, even if

---

1. See discussion in *TAPS*, 34–64, especially its framing on p. 37: "Yet prayer, penance, and monastic reform were not Teresa's only ways of realizing her desire to do missionary work. . . . In the end, Teresa expressed her desire to convert souls by her literary works, whose purpose was less to describe her own experiences than to teach and compel. Yet she encountered as much resistance to her literary endeavors as to her reform efforts." See also, Jodi Bilinkoff, "Teresa of Avila: Woman with a Mission," in Emily Michelson et al., eds, *A Linking of Heaven and Earth: Studies in Religious and Cultural History in Honor of Carlos M. N. Eire* (Burlington, VT: Ashgate, 2013); Barbara Mujica, *Teresa de Avila: Lettered Woman* (Nashville, TN: Vanderbilt University Press, 2009), esp. 44–102; Alison Weber, "Spiritual Administration: Gender and Discernment in the Carmelite Reform" in *Sixteenth Century Journal* Vol. 31, No. 1 (Spring 2000), 123–46.

we tend to think of Teresa as the more active of the two. But John was just as much of a "restless, disobedient gadabout"—the famous and scathing words used by papal nuncio Felipe Sega to describe Teresa—moving from foundation to foundation, constantly serving the reform.[2] After his early years at Duruelo, he was appointed rector of the Carmelite house of studies at Alcalá (1570–71). Then, he served as the spiritual director to the community of the Encarnación. In 1578, after his escape from prison, he became prior of El Calvario, in the south of Spain, and spiritual director for the Discalced nuns at Beas. This is where he came to know Teresa's close companion Ana de Jesús, to whom he eventually dedicated his *Spiritual Canticle*. In 1582, he became prior in Granada, and in 1585, he became the vicar provincial of the whole of Andalusia. In that same year, he traveled to Málaga, Lisbon, Seville, Pastrana, and other communities, tending to administrative matters within the order, and in 1586, his travels were even more extensive. His work as prior of Segovia in 1588 must have seemed light, even though it involved building an entire new monastery there. It is humbling to imagine him writing such sublime poetry and reflection about intimate partnership with God around such intense demands on his time. And in the end, his keen commitment to the reform which put him in opposition to decisions made by the Vicar General of the Discalced, Nicolás Doria, in 1590, led to his reclusion in the south of Spain, where he died, simply and in a place where he was virtually unknown.[3]

As we consider the legacy of these two extraordinary human beings, it is important to continue to hold together these two critical (and compatible) vocations: authors of profound mystical texts as well as administrators of a massive reform. It would be tempting (and it would suit our contemporary biases about what contemplation is) to

2. "Fémina inquieta y andariega, desobediente y contumaz que, bajo el color de la devoción, inventa malas doctrinas . . . ("a restless, disobedient and obstinate gadabout, who, under the guise of devotion spreads evil teachings . . .") Felipe Sega reportedly spoke of Teresa this way in conversation with Juan de Jesús, as recorded by Francisco de Santa María in *Reforma de los Descalzos de Nuestra Señora del Carmen de la primitive observancia* vol. 1 (Madrid, 1644), book 4, chapter 30, paragraph 2. Cited in Angel Fernández Collado, *Gergorio XIII y Felipe II en la nunciatura de Felipe Sega (1577–1581): Aspectos politico, jurisdiccional y de reforma* (Toledo: Kadmos, 1991), 345n3.
3. For a summary of John's final years, see "General Introduction" in CWJC, 23–26.

remember them only as significant and accomplished writers, which they were. But that is not how their contemporaries knew them. They saw amazingly *active* and *engaged* people, alive with love—a love which, in Teresa, pulses with vitality and one which, in John, gently refreshed and restored people whenever they conversed with him. Even today, we can feel traces of John's own tenderness in the delicate lyricism of his writing and sense the passionate bravura of Teresa in her prose. I make this point, in part, because our studies of them often consider only one facet of their giftedness, not the complex integration of gifts that each of them accomplished, nor their continual expression of that integration on a day-to-day basis. It is worth noting that their profound "busy-ness" and responsibility (which surely would rival or surpass any of ours) did not pull them from a space and disposition of deep kindness. This ought to be at least as instructive to us as their theological and spiritual insights.

As all authors know, books begin to take on a life of their own, apart from ours. As we begin to consider the independent life of Teresa and John's written works, though, we see, for at least the first 50 years of the reception of their words, a continued integration of their writings and the larger movement of reform to which they had dedicated themselves. Even as we see continuing misunderstanding and resistance. It may be that we see more resistance to Teresa the author than to John the author, and we see more misunderstanding of John the author than of Teresa the author. This thesis merits more consideration.

The substantial work that has been done to explore women's lack of teaching authority[4] leaves little room to doubt that Teresa had significantly more to overcome in realizing her vocation as a writer than John did. For example, she wrote two versions of both *The Book of Her Life* (1562 and 1565) and *The Way of Perfection* (1565 and c. 1566),[5]

---

4. In addition to scholars working specifically on Teresa and issues of gender and authority (e.g. myself, Elena Carrera, Barbara Mujica, Carole Slade, Alison Weber), there is the fine work of Sarah Coakley, Grace Jantzen, Barbara Newman, Ulrike Wiethaus, and others.

5. Daniel de Pablo Maroto believes that the second redaction was written closer to 1569, citing in particular, the work of Tomás de la Cruz, *Camino de perfección*, II (Roma: Teresianum, 1966), 15–30, 95–103. For a careful comparison of the differences in the two versions, see *TAPS*, 86–97.

and in each case, she responded carefully to both the spirit and the letter of the censor's comments to her first drafts. But despite her scrupulous consultation with spiritual experts and their approval of her way of life, the *The Book of Her Life* was held by the Inquisition after Domingo Bánez's official assessment of its contents in July of 1575.[6] Teresa did not take kindly to the sequestration of the *Life* and approached Inquisitor General Gaspar de Quiroga through a third party to have it released. But although Quiroga reviewed it and found nothing wrong with it, even asking her why she had not yet founded a convent in Madrid, Teresa did not receive the manuscript back. It was shortly after this exchange with Quiroga that Teresa decided to write the *Interior Castle*, which then replaced and even superseded her previous work.[7] The Inquisition held the manuscript for twelve years and only relinquished it upon the insistence of Ana de Jesús, founder of the Discalced Carmelite convent in Madrid, who asked that it be included in the first publication of Teresa's complete works, edited by Luis de León in 1588.

Ironically, we should actually be quite grateful for the Inquisition's actions against *The Book of Her Life*, because shortly afterward, out of a space of even greater spiritual maturity and integration (and directly in response to the sequestration of the *Life*[8]), Teresa set out to write what became her mystical *tour de force*—the *Interior Castle*. In light of the recent confiscation of the *Life* and the fact that Teresa had had to defend herself in a separate inquisitional investigation in Seville in

---

6. For a summary of this proceeding and analysis of Bánez's assessment and its impact, see *TAPS*, 49–52.
7. Teresa had her friend Luisa de la Cerda approach Gaspar de Quiroga to inquire about the status of the book, which he took the time to read personally. As Teresa relates to her brother Lorenzo in February 1577, "he told Lady Luisa that there was nothing that the inquisitors should be concerned about in it; in fact it was not dangerous but helpful; and he asked her why I had not founded a convent yet in Madrid." See Carta 183:14 (27–28 February 1577) in OC 1576–80 at 1578. See also *TAPS*, 51–52.
8. See *Entering*, 11–15, especially the conversation between Teresa and fellow reformer Jerónimo Gracián, in which the two of them decide together that she should "write down what you remember, and other things, and write another book, and explain the basic teachings without identifying the person who has experienced what you are writing about..." as noted in Jerónimo Gracián, *Anotaciones al P. Ribera* in Antonio de San Joaquín, *Año teresiano, diario histórico, panegyrico moral, en que se descubren las virtudes, sucesos y maravaillas de la seráphica y mystica Doctora de la Iglesia Santa Teresa de Jesús*, 12 vols. (Madrid, 1733-69), 7:149. Note here that Teresa is being called a "mystical doctor" of the church many centuries before she was officially declared so by Paul VI.

1575–76, where she had been accused of misconduct and unorthodox spiritual practices, it is hard not to see the very writing of the *Interior Castle* as a prophetic act of resistance, despite its complex rhetoric of obedience.[9] In any case, Teresa's long history of struggle for authority as a writer and spiritual teacher positioned her to craft the *Interior Castle* in such a way that it escaped any significant criticism.

Teresa's orthodoxy and authority were challenged after her death, shortly after the release of her *Complete Works* by Guillermo Foquel in Salamanca in 1588. Again, the concerns seemed to be at least as much the audacity of public circulation of works by a woman as the actual content of her writings. The posthumous wave of criticism, led by the Dominican Alonso de la Fuente and others, began by arguing that it was *"preter naturam"* ("against nature") for the doctrine contained in the book to be taught by a woman, a line of argument that others after him followed.[10] Teresa's orthodoxy was vigorously defended by Luis de León and Antonio de Quevedo, another Augustinian. The two of them located Teresa squarely in a much larger tradition of Christian mysticism, citing the affinity of her teachings with those of Richard of St. Victor, Bernard of Clairvaux, Bonaventure, Jean Gerson, and others. The two men also employed a hagiographical strategy that stressed Teresa's exceptionalism, effectively suggesting that *this* woman, *this* time could teach, but only because she was directly inspired by the Holy Spirit.[11] This view of Teresa, which effectively rejected her agency and authority as a writer and theologian, was a persistent theme for centuries, reinforced within the iconographic tradition, especially as it moved into the age of the baroque. By suggesting that Teresa was inspired directly by the Holy Spirit, their strategy *did* resolve the question of her orthodoxy, which led to the rapid diffusion of her works, especially once she was canonized in 1622. Although popular in

---

9. See discussion of the genesis of the *Interior Castle* text in *TAPS*, 61–62 and *Entering*, 11–15. See also Alison Weber, *Teresa of Avila and the Rhetoric of Femininity*, 98–122.

10. See Alonso de La Fuente's 1589 Memorial to the Inquisition transcribed in Enrique Llamas, *Santa Teresa y la Inquisición Española* (Madrid: Editorial de Espiritualidad, 1972), 396–97. See discussion in *TAPS*, 114–44, esp. 118–23.

11. For a more careful analysis of Teresa's canonization process and its various stages, see *TAPS*, 145–66.

many quarters, John's writings did not gain such rapid approval—and his canonization process may have been slowed, as a result.

Meanwhile, the second realm of their reform efforts—that of monastic foundations—continued to flourish through the 1580s, 1590s, and 1600s. The women who were at the core of Carmelite leadership during Teresa's lifetime—María de San José, Ana de Jesús, and Ana de San Bartolomé—were greatly responsible for extending her message in the decades after Teresa's death. María de San José, probably the most educated and spirited of Teresa's initial collaborators, kept the Teresian reform alive under persecution in Seville, where she served as prioress during the rough years of the 1570s; then, she was transferred to Lisbon, where she served as prioress until 1598.[12] Ana de Jesús maintained contact and collaboration with John of the Cross in Granada through 1586. Then, both of them went to Madrid to establish the first discalced Carmelite convent there. While prioress there, she worked to retrieve Teresa's *Life* for inclusion in the publication of her *Complete Works*, prepared by Luis de León. She served as prioress in Salamanca beginning in 1596, and then, went with Ana de San Bartolomé and others to Paris in 1604 to begin the Carmelite reform in France. Ana de San Bartolomé, who served as Teresa's nurse and secretary from 1577 until the time of her death in 1582, also went to Paris in 1604, where, in addition to serving as the prioress in Paris, she founded two houses in France, Pontoise and Tours. She later founded a house in Antwerp in 1612, where she died in 1626. She left behind an *Autobiography*, *Conferences*, poetry, a *Defense of the Teresian Inheritance* and over 600 extant letters.[13] The sisters' success, as writers and as

12. See Alison Weber, "María de San José: Saint Teresa's Difficult Daughter" in Christopher C. Wilson, *The Heirs of St. Teresa of Avila: Defenders and Disseminators of the Founding Mother's Legacy* (Washington, DC: Institute of Carmelite Studies, 2006), 1–20. See also her important study of María, coupled with a translation of María's *Book of Recreations*, which provides important historical and spiritual material, in *For the Hour of Recreation by María de San José* (Chicago: University of Chicago, 2002).

13. Ana de San Bartolomé's autobiography is available in Ana de San Bartolomé, *Autobiography and Other Writings*, trans. Darcy Donahue (Chicago: University of Chicago, 2008). Jerónimo Gracián also wrote a *Life* of Ana de San Bartolomé, formally titled *Espíritu y revelaciones y manera de proceder de la Madre Ana de san Bartolomé examinado por el P. Fr. Jerónimo Gracián de la Madre de Dios su confessor*, first published in 1933 in Silverio de Santa Teresa, ed., *Biblioteca Mística Carmelitana* (Burgos: Monte Carmelo, 1933), 17.

reformers, was further testimony to the orthodoxy of Teresa and her movement, and they promulgated Teresa's teachings in all the ways that they could.

Teresa's major trilogy—her *Life*, the *Way of Perfection*, and her *Interior Castle*—were translated into French as early as 1601 and began to have an immediate impact on French piety and spirituality. Both Francis de Sales (1567–1622) and Jeanne de Chantal (1572–1641) were heavily influenced by Teresa and important in bringing her reforms into France, by supporting Carmelite convents and by diffusing her ideas into their own writings. Francis' own *Treatise on the Love of God* cites Teresa frequently and with admiration and affection, indicating a spiritual kinship between the two that has been studied.[14] After meeting Francis de Sales in 1604, the widowed Jeanne de Chantal dedicated herself to spiritual growth and founded the religious order of the Visitation in 1610. In her writings, she reveals Teresa's influence on her, but her focus is on the development of the virtues of charity, humility, and obedience. Pierre de Bérulle also incorporated elements of Teresa's thought into the French School. Eventually, however, he and Ana de San Bartolomé locked horns on how to authentically live out Teresa's charism, leading Ana to abandon France and spread the Teresian reform in the Spanish Netherlands.[15] By 1625, there were 37 discalced Carmelite convents in France alone. This movement fed a counter-Reformation agenda to revitalize Catholicism in France through a deepening of piety and prayer.

The overall trend in seventeenth-century France was to emphasize abandonment of the will as a development of the virtue of humility. This was a caricature of Teresa's theological anthropology, made worse when reinforced by interpretations of John's notion of the "passivity" of the soul after the publication of the first edition of John of the

---

14. See, for example, Joseph Chorpenning, "St. Joseph in the Spirituality of Teresa of Avila and of Francis de Sales: Convergences and Divergences" in Wilson, *Heirs of St. Teresa*, 123–40. See also Elisabeth Stopp, "Spanish Links: St. Francis de Sales and St. Teresa of Avila" in Elisabeth Stopp, *A Man to Heal Differences: Essays and Talks on St. Francis de Sales* (Philadelphia: St. Joseph's University, 1997), 171–82. For more on both figures and Teresa's influence in France more generally, see Alphonse Vermeylen, *Sainte Thérèse en France au XVIIe siècle 1600-1660* (Louvain: Publications Universitaires, 1958).

15. See "Blessed Anne of St. Barthelomew" in Wilson, *The Heirs of St. Teresa of Avila*.

Cross' works in French in 1621. Subsequent editions of John's works circulated throughout the century—1627, 1628, 1641, 1652, 1665, and 1695. Teresa and John's affectivity, John's lyricism, the malleability of Teresa's self-representation and her lengthy discussions of humility, all proved to be helpful to the growth of a spiritual school that cultivated virtue, piety, charity, a strong and committed relationship with Christ, and devotion to Mary and the saints and served a post-Tridentine context of catechism, clericalism, and mission.

Back in Spain, John of the Cross' works hit a major snag when the Alcalá edition of John's works (published in 1618, without the *Spiritual Canticle*) was denounced to the Spanish Inquisition. Although John's orthodoxy was ably defended by Basilio Ponce de León, nephew of Luis de León and esteemed in his own right as a theologian and professor at the University of Salamanca, interpretation of John's teachings about the "activity" and "passivity" of the soul continued to be a problem throughout the seventeenth century. Like Teresa's apologists a few decades earlier, de León situated John within a larger mystical tradition—showing his compatibility with the Victorine tradition, for example—and now used Teresa's canonization and the growth of the Carmelite order as proof of the spiritual benefits of John's teachings.

John was beatified in 1675, a profound vindication of his orthodoxy, but this was the same year that Miguel de Molinos (1628–96) published his *Spiritual Guide*, encouraging and popularizing interior prayer, especially the "prayer of quiet." Condemnation of Molinos in 1687 and controversy over Jeanne de Guyon (1648–1717), who states her admiration for Teresa in her *Autobiography*, exemplify ongoing concern about whether or not Teresa and John's mystical teachings could be properly received by a public that clearly wanted effective models of spirituality. Expansion of Teresa and John's thought into the Americas began in 1604 with the establishment of a discalced Carmelite convent in Puebla. In the Americas, too, Carmelite convents were seen to support missionary efforts to convert Native Americans through prayer. As more recent studies of the writings of Teresa's heirs have shown, Teresa's influence trickled through prayer and devotional practices even as it opened up literary genres to other women writers.[16] In his review of the Teresian legacy, Christopher C. Wilson writes, "Through prayer, dispensation of spiritual advice, acceptance of novices, and the placement of churches beside their convents, female monastic communities played a key role in cultivating a relatively young American church. The propagation of Teresa's legacy, therefore, was a global enterprise."[17] Recent studies of the lives of Hispanic nuns suggest that Teresa's *Life* provided women not simply with a model of prayer practice around which to pattern their lives, but also with rhetorical strategies of self-expression that allowed them greater roles as teachers and reformers in their own right.[18]

Teresa's canonization in 1622 was a validation of her orthodoxy and signaled an authoritative Catholic re-appropriation of the mystical tradition. However, Teresa's identity as a canonized saint served to separate the practical relevance of her teachings on prayer from the ordinary experience of the faithful. Ironically, the church's official endorsement of Teresa's way made the mystical life appear far less accessible than Teresa actually taught that it was. Teresa's insights, whether theological or practical/pastoral, were rendered functionally irrelevant because now, the focus of attention was on venerating (and perhaps imitating) her as a model of religious practice and not on reading, digesting, and assimilating her teachings. Given the controversy surrounding her life, we should recognize that

> Teresa's canonization was not at all inevitable. It should be seen as a result of three factors: a rather dogged campaign on her behalf by the Spanish crown and several nobles; the successful construction of a female role model who was able to represent most of the virtues associated with femininity while overcoming the negative attributes associated with

---

16. See Electa Arenal and Stacey Schlau, *Untold Sisters: Hispanic Nuns in Their Own Works* (Albuquerque: University of New Mexico, 1989).

17. Christopher C. Wilson, *The Heirs of St. Teresa*, 3–4. For further understanding of the global influence of Teresa on her readers, see Jodi Bilinkoff, "Touched by Teresa: Readers and their Responses, 1588-1750" in Ibid., 107–22.

18. See, for example, Clara A. Herrera, "Influences of St. Catherine of Siena and St. Teresa of Avila on the Columbian Nun Jerónima Nava y Saavedra" in Hilaire Kalendorf, ed., *A New Companion to Hispanic Mysticism* (Leiden: Brill, 2010), 253–72 at 265: "Jerónima's exposition shows techniques used by Teresa, especially in her *Vida*, to relate her remarkable visions and (as Jerónima would do later) to fashion herself as teacher, reformer, and intercessor before God."

womanhood; and, perhaps most important, the Roman Catholic Church's endorsement of the mystical way as an important part of the Counter-Reformation identity. Thus we must distinguish between Teresa as she embodied the Christian life and the growing construction of Teresa as a Christian type to be emulated.[19]

Teresa's canonization did not necessarily result in the integration of her thought in the canon of *theological* teachings, whether in Catholic or in wider Christian thought. In fact, in many ways, the same subjectivity that gave Teresa experiential authority also served to marginalize her theological impact. The reasons for this are more contextual than anything, but it is nonetheless lamentable that the immediate reception to Teresa's ideas, after so much struggle simply to make sure that they survived and were accessible, was that they moved again toward the margins as epistemological shifts relegated subjectivity to liminal space. In his analysis of how mystical thought "becomes private piety," Mark McIntosh argues that

> . . . [B]y the time of Teresa of Avila (1515-82) this drama of the inner world had become a necessary substitute for a cosmos that, in de Certeau's memorable phrase, "is no longer perceived as *spoken* by God, that . . . has become opacified, objectified, and detached from its supposed speaker." The inner self becomes the temporary substitute for the more public "speech" of God. . . . For Teresa, this "interior mansion" becomes the imaginal realm in which the divine speech can still be heard, but now the language of that speech is constituted by the inner movements of the soul. The soul itself is "but the inarticulate echo of an unknown Subject," thus it needs a dramatic imaginary inner stage upon which to act out and narrate the mysterious and inexpressible touch of "Unknownness." And so, coincident with the apparent divine withdrawal from the cosmos, mysticism in modernity also withdraws into this inner castle, the world of the inner self—a world whose claims to wisdom, authority and truth could easily be marginalized by religious and academic authorities...[20]

Teresa's subjectivity, however, is not simply relegated to an inner world. Rather, her passionate experience of God is glorified through

---

19. TAPS, 146–47.
20. Mark McIntosh, *Mystical Theology: The Integrity of Spirituality and Theology* (Malden, MA: Blackwell, 1998) 69; cf. Michel de Certeau, *The Mystic Fable*, vol. 1, The Sixteenth and Seventeenth Centuries, trans. Michael B. Smith (Chicago: University of Chicago, 1992), 188–90.

representations of the "Ecstasy of St. Teresa," the most famous of which, of course, was that of Gian Lorenzo Bernini in 1652. Placed in the Cornaro chapel of Santa Maria della Vitoria in Rome (where it replaced a previous image of St. Paul in ecstasy), the work takes a private, intimate encounter with God that Teresa says that she experienced "in the intimate depths of my being"[21] and places it on public display. In fact, embedded in the composition of the image are four life-size figures who appear on the side walls. They are male members of the Cornaro family, looking on and talking about the moment as if it were a scene at the theatre.[22] Thus, Teresa as a theologian becomes subject both to the marginalization of her subjectivity and its theatrical display; a thing of "pious curiosity" or even prurient interest. Both inclinations follow McIntosh's description of a trend over the next centuries in which, he writes:

> "[T]he mystic" has, in Western culture more generally, become something of a marginal eccentric at best, whose peculiar inner experience (to use Underhill's words) of "unimaginable tension and delight" has come to seem a thing of pious curiosity perhaps, but clearly of little relevance for the serious task of academic theology.[23]

By the late seventeenth century, Teresa had become, for many, a symbol of effusive piety or an object of pious devotion. Although she continued to be a venerated spiritual mother within the Carmelite tradition at least, she was not truly known as a person, as a thinker, as a spiritual companion, or as a woman who spoke frankly and encouraged a deep familiarity in our relationship with God.[24] Throughout the

---

21. See her description in L 29:13, where she describes fire at the tip of a dart entering her heart several times and reaching into her center ("me llegaba a las entrañas"). Some (e.g. Peers) have translated "entrañas" literally as "entrails;" others translate it "heart."
22. For more on the image, see Robert Harbison, *Reflections on Baroque* (Chicago: University of Chicago, 2000).
23. McIntosh, *Mystical Theology*, 69. In fact, after Bernini, Teresa seems to have gotten caught somewhere between "pious curiosity" and voyeuristic fetishism.
24. The primary concern of authors in the seventeenth century was keeping alive Carmelite prayer practice, as it had been taught by Teresa and John. Thus, the primary genres developed were prayer manuals, spiritual chronicles and other devotional works. Cordula van Wyhe, for example, has traced the influence of the *Idea Vitae Teresianae Iconibus Symbolica Expressa*, produced in the Low Countries as "a manual for novices needing instruction in the path to spiritual maturity." Eleven copies of this work survive; it focuses on mortification, the practice of virtue, mental prayer, and supernatural prayer. See Cordula van Wyhe, "The Teresian Mystic Life and its Visual

eighteenth and nineteenth centuries, however, Teresa and John's works themselves (as opposed to the pious traditions around them) remained to be discovered, often by individuals who were looking for spiritual guides through the reading of mystical texts. Such was the case with Isaac Hecker (1819–88), for example, founder of the Paulists, who was strongly influenced by John of the Cross as an integral part of his spiritual development and continued to read John throughout his life.[25] By the late nineteenth and early twentieth centuries, Teresa and John re-emerged as some of the most helpful figures in the spiritual formation of Catholic clergy and vowed religious. New English translations of their works (e.g. David Lewis' two-volume edition of John in 1864, his translation of Teresa's *Life* in 1870, and his translation of the *Book of the Foundations* in 1871; Teresa's *Interior Castle* in 1921 by the Benedictines of Stanbrook) contributed to wider knowledge of their contributions.

Teresa and John (but, most particularly, John) took even more prominent place as the normative teachers of the mystical life after Evelyn Underhill's influential *Mysticism: A Study of the Nature and Development of Man's Spiritual Consciousness*, first published in 1911. Underhill, a novelist and poet deeply attracted to spiritual growth, attempted, in this work, to create a compendium of phenomenological insights from writers of the mystical tradition. In the second half of the work, she constructed a "map" of the mystical life, drawn primarily from the three elements of the mystical life (purgation, illumination, and union) and enhanced by significant material from John of the Cross. Although this book was widely considered an (by some "the") authoritative "study" of mysticism throughout the twentieth century, Underhill had no theological training and was largely self-educated. She was most interested in the subjective dimensions of spiritual experience and the extent to which the mystical life was a practical, transformative phenomenon, and she devoted herself to the work of

---

Representation in the Low Countries" in Cordula van Wyhe, ed., *Female Monasticism in Early Modern Europe* (Burlington, VT: Ashgate, 2008), 173.

25. See Steven Payne, "The Influence of John of the Cross in the United States" in Steven Payne, ed., *John of the Cross* (Washington, DC: Institute of Carmelite Studies, 1992), 170–73.

spiritual growth and to conversations with spiritual teachers until, gradually, she became one herself. *Mysticism* sold over a million copies and made the mystical tradition as a phenomenon and spirituality as a way of life widely accessible, especially to Protestants, in ways that they had not been before. Underhill herself was widely acclaimed as a sincere spiritual seeker; she sought spiritual direction from Friedrich von Hügel, corresponded with Rabindranath Tagore, and was invited to give the Upton lectures in philosophy of religion at Manchester College, Oxford.[26] Underhill's work gives lay readers some basic toeholds into the subjectivity of John of the Cross, and exposed English-speaking readers for the first time to "the dark night of the soul" as a spiritual concept and experience.

Underhill's treatment of John of the Cross is at least sympathetic to his intent and appreciative of his charism. Other authors are even more simplistic in their review of his thought and end up being rather dismissive: "Unnatural," "quietistic," "consummate ascetic,"[27] with "a terrible view of life and duty."[28] In his review of John's influence in the U.S., Steven Payne acknowledges: "It would be safe to say that authors such as R. M. Bucke, William James and Evelyn Underhill have played an important role in gaining for John, if not a place of honor, at least a serious hearing among American psychologists and philosophers of religion."[29] Regrettably, however, the characterization of John in each of these authors is seriously flawed, in that there is no attempt to understand the insights John gives us into the nature of God or the nature of the human person. Further, much American scholarship has been deeply influenced by early depictions of John's "dark night of the soul," without any real engagement of John's overall thought and without approaching the whole of his corpus in John's native Castilian.

---

26. Her lectures there were published under the title *The Life of the Spirit and the Life of Today* (1922).
27. Thus, Robert Vaughn, *Hours With the Mystics: A Contribution to the History of Religious Opinion,* (New York, NY: Charles Scribner's Sons, 1893), 2:149–52, 183–97, summarized in Steven Payne, "The Influence of John of the Cross in the United States," 174–75.
28. Thus, William Ralph Inge, *Christian Mysticism* (New York, NY: Meridian, 1956), 230, cited in Payne, "The Influence of John of the Cross in the United States," 175.
29. Payne, "The Influence of John of the Cross in the United States," 176.

No attempt to appreciate John could be entirely satisfactory in translation.

Finally, and by way of transition, we should note John of the Cross' influence on Dorothy Day and Thomas Merton, who, in turn, open up wider interest in their teachings in the second half of the twentieth century. Merton, in particularly, devoted significant attention to John in his early *Ascent to Truth* (1951), and he articulates, in a preliminary way and perhaps for the first time, the significance of Teresa and John's place in the counter-Reformation and their complementarity (though not their mutual influence on one another and their true collaboration in the 1570s), when he writes:

> Teresa herself had a clearly apostolic notion of the contemplative life. She believed that her nuns, by their lives of prayer and sacrifice, would do much to atone for the religious confusion of sixteenth-century Europe, to save souls, and to preserve the unity of the Catholic Church. It is extremely significant that one of the finest fruits of the Catholic Counter-Reformation should have been an order in which contemplative prayer in the strict sense was not only emphasized but adopted as an end.
>
> When Saint John of the Cross joined Saint Teresa in 1568 and began, in his turn, to lay the foundations for a reform of the Carmelite Friars, a new note was added: the priests of the order would not only practice contemplation, they would also preach the ways of interior prayer and enable souls, by their direction, to arrive at a certain degree of contemplation, not only in convents but even in the world.[30]

Probably the most competent intellectuals and practitioners of the contemplative tradition, especially as that tradition comes into dialogue with the modern world, both were well-positioned to appreciate John's substantive contributions; however, neither of them retrieves either John's theological power or his capacity to speak, in an integrated way, to social concerns.[31] However, the spiritual authority

---

30. Thomas Merton, *Ascent to Truth* (New York: Harcourt Brace, 1951), 328.
31. See Payne's assessment, with which I thoroughly agree: " . . . [D]uring his early years as a Trappist, Merton did as much as anyone in this century to arouse American interest in John of the Cross. It is only unfortunate that he never seemed to have appreciated the full power of Sanjuanist mysticism to incorporate the very social justice and inter-religious concerns which Merton himself later helped raise, and which have been more deeply explored by those who have followed in his footsteps (e.g. Daniel Berrigan, William Johnston, and others)."

of these two major figures, Day and Merton, as well as their significant accomplishments, as writers, teachers, and human beings, contributed to a re-appropriation of the legacy of Teresa and John that we are still accomplishing today.

Resurgence of Interest and Re-Appropriation Toward the End of the Twentieth Century

In the latter half of the twentieth century, several developments in the understanding of Teresa and John made it possible for us to recognize them as theologians in their own right and not just saints or spiritual teachers. In many ways, these developments were necessary in order for us to comprehend the theological impact of their lives and for those theological contributions to have ongoing transformative impact. Certainly, these interpretations caused huge shifts in how we view the theological landscape of the sixteenth century, and therefore, in how we draw the map. These shifts were so dramatic that it seems incredible, today, to remember that in the early 1990s, when I was first writing my dissertation, one still had to argue (sometimes quite vigorously, at that) that Teresa was a theologian! Teresa and John's normative situation in the theological canon is actually something that had to be accomplished over the course of centuries.

Even the declaration of Teresa as a doctor of the Roman Catholic Church in 1970 was of perhaps less import theologically than we might expect. Her title, "Doctor of Prayer," emphasizes her role as a spiritual teacher, and it definitively overcame the hurdle of her teaching authority. But the popular image of Teresa enraptured, the deep subjectivity of her self-expression, and the inability to recognize her capacity to function as a systematic theologian within the literary genres that she employed continued to challenge our appreciation of her theological contributions. Interestingly, it was historians and literary critics who paved the way toward a deeper synthesis of the spiritual and theological synthesis that has been so deeply needed.

The first step toward this re-appropriation of their theological impact was due to the scholarship of historians, who revealed the socio-economic realities of both Teresa and John. In 1946, Narciso Alonso Cortes dropped a bombshell in the *Boletín de la Real Academia Española* under the innocuous title, "Pleitos de los Cepedas." This article, which reviewed the lawsuits of Teresa's family as they strove to claim their rights as *hidalgos*, revealed the Inquisitional verdict against Teresa's grandfather, Juan Sánchez, for "judaizing" and situated Teresa squarely in the marginality of "new Christians."[32] This discovery opened up new questions about how to read her "autobiography" and how to understand the reform to which the two of them dedicated their lives.

Because Teresa had so easily erased significant details of her life, literary critics, beginning with Victor García de la Concha and Rosa Rossi, interrogated Teresa's "rustic style" and revealed the inadequacy of centuries of interpreting Teresa as the passive recipient of divine revelation.[33] Alison Weber's influential *Teresa of Avila and the Rhetoric of Femininity* (1990) moved this line of interpretation forward by articulating the rhetorical strategies at work in Teresa's writings, and my *Teresa of Avila and the Politics of Sanctity* (1995) situated Teresa more clearly in the ecclesiastical framework as a female theologian writing around the Spanish Inquisition's suspicion of mental prayer and scrutiny of mystical texts. These instincts, reinforced by the trend toward a more nuanced approach to contextual theology[34], have made

---

32. Narciso Alonso Cortes, "Pleitos de los Cepeda" in *Boletín de la Real Academia Española* 25 (1946): 85–110. An explosion of scholarship followed, including: Teófanes Egido, "La familia judía de Santa Teresa," *Studia Zamorensia* 3 (1982): 449–79; José Gómez Menor, *El Linaje familiar de Santa Teresa y de San Juan de la Cruz: Sus parientes toledanos* (Toledo, 1970); Francisco Márquez Villanueva, "Santa Teresa y el linaje" in *Espiritualidad y literature en el siglo XVI* (Madrid, 1968); and Homero Seris, "Nueva genealogía de Santa Teresa" in *Nueva Revista de Filología Hispánica* 10 (1965): 363–84.
33. Victor García de la Concha, *El arte literario de Santa Teresa* (Barcelona: Ariel, 1978) and Rosa Rossi, *Teresa de Avila: Biografía de una escritora*, trans. Marieta Gargatagli (Barcelona: ICARIA, 1984).
34. See, e.g. Teófanes Egido's call for a "new biography" of Teresa, one that would not "perpetuate the image of the saint isolated in a greatness that never manages to situate itself within social, economic, political, and psychological conditions" in "El tratamiento historiográfico de Santa Teresa: Inercias y revisiones" in *Perfil histórico de Santa Teresa*, ed. Teófanes Egido (Madrid: Editorial de Espiritualidad, 1981), 22. Egido responded to his own call to arms in 1986 with *El linaje judeoconverso de Santa Teresa: pleito de hidalguía de los Cepeda* (Madrid: Editorial de Espiritualidad, 1986) and has recently published *Sobre Teresa de Jesús* with José Jiménez Lozano. Efrén de la Madre de Dios and Otger Steggink's massive *Tiempo y vida de Santa Teresa* was another worthy response to the integration of historical knowledge to this re-appropriation of Teresa. It was first published in 1986 in the Biblioteca de Autores Cristianos series, and is now in its third edition (1996).

it impossible not to consider Teresa a rigorous theologian in her own right.[35]

As I have attempted to outline so far, there any many factors that have contributed to a partial and still quite incomplete reception and integration of Teresa and John's legacy. Given the sheer number of publications and frequent reference to one or the other of them, this would seem puzzling. Indeed, it might seem that by now we have surely exhausted anything that might be said about them. But 500 years after Teresa's birth and with more interest in Teresa and John than ever, we are just now coming into the creative possibilities that their spiritual-theological synthesis holds. For too long, we have been kept from apprehending and applying it to our day and age. In fact, if we continue to cling to some of the binaries (theological vs. spiritual, intellectual vs. affective, contemplative vs. apostolic, Catholic vs. Protestant) that have characterized our approaches this far, we may not stretch toward the God Teresa and John knew—the One who is beyond name, yet who tenderly calls us out of ourselves and wants to hold us in an embrace of unfathomable kindness. Ultimately, it is God's self-revelation as the lover and companion who is constantly surprising us with consolation and delight, humbling us with immense attentiveness, wanting to come alive in us and in our world that we stand to lose, if we do not heed the teachings of Teresa and John. And this would be at least as much of a "pity," as Teresa says, as "that we do not understand ourselves nor do we know who we are,"[36] since, for both of them, God was experienced as the single compelling energy capable of providing meaning and direction, no matter what dissonance life meted out. As we look out upon a world grown even more chaotic than ever, their understanding, both of the divine and of human nature is more critical than ever.

In honor of the 500th anniversary of Teresa's birth, many conferences drew together people who have spent decades walking

---

35. Thus, for example, Barbara Mujica, *Teresa de Ávila: Lettered Woman* (Nashville, TN: Vanderbilt University Press, 2009). See also J. Mary Luti, *Teresa of Avila's Way* (Collegeville, MN: Liturgical Press, 1991).

36. See IC I:1:2 and above, p. 19.

with Teresa and John. These convocations demonstrated clearly that the legacy of Teresa and John is more alive than ever. It seems appropriate to end this volume by delineating briefly some of the avenues for deeper exploration and integration going forward.

If Teresa and John show us that we are created by and for love, they also show us that such love is radically practical—not theoretical, not abstract, not formed in our imagination as we consider what "we might do," but rather, measured in terms of what we actually do. "Love is never idle," Teresa reminds us, "and such a failure would be a very bad sign."[37] Their insistence that love is fruitful parallels Pope Francis' reminder to the Christian community as a whole, that "knows that God has taken the initiative and has loved us first (cf. 1 John 4:19)" should "boldly take the initiative, go out to others, seek those who have fallen away, stand at the crossroads and welcome the outcast," especially because "God wants us to be fruitful."[38] What might this look like? To use Teresa's yardstick, any statement or act of faith would have to inspire a more intentional and thoughtful love in others. The quality of our faith (as well as the quality of our humanity) would be measured in terms of our capacity to "enkindle love"—that is, to participate in and diffuse new life in a dying world, like the phoenix, who, all burnt up, rises from the very same ash.[39] Teresa and John

---

37. IC V:4:10, cf. p. 51, above.

38. Cf., Francis, *Joy of the Gospel*, par. 24: "An evangelizing community knows that God has taken the initiative and has loved us first (cf. 1 John 4:19), and therefore we can move forward, boldly take the initiative, go out to others, seek those who have fallen away, stand at the crossroads and welcome the outcast. An evangelizing community gets involved by word and deed in people's daily lives; it bridges distances, and it embraces human life, touching the suffering flesh of Christ in others... Faithful to the Lord's gift, it also bears fruit. An evangelizing community is always concerned with fruit, because God wants us to be fruitful. Finally, an evangelizing community is filled with joy; it knows how to rejoice always. It celebrates at every small victory, every step forward in the work of evangelization."

39. The metaphor of the phoenix does not have the same primacy in Teresa's work that the castle, the fountain or the caterpillar and butterfly do, but its capacity to convey the resurrected life that we live in and through Christ is important enough that she uses it in her *Life*, and then repeats it in her *Interior Castle*, in case readers are unable to read the *Life*. See L 29:23 and IC VI:4:3: "Totally burnt up like the phoenix, now it remains renewed." In John, the phoenix is the best way to convey the impact of the soul's initial "wounding" experience of God's love, as he writes in his commentary on stanza one of the *Spiritual Canticle*: " . . . [B]esides the other many different kinds of visits that God grants the soul, in which God tenderizes and raises it up in love, God also gives it enkindling touches of love, which, like fiery darts, pierce and open it and leave it completely cauterized by the fire of love. These openings are rightly called "wounds of love," about which the soul speaks here. They inflame the will in affection so much that the soul is afire in the flame

remind us that the point, not just of faith, but also of being human, is to be drawn into loving activity—godly activity—through our relationship with the divine. Not only are we transformed by that relationship (as if that, in itself, would not be enough), but we, too, are then easily and joyfully drawn into the work of renewing the world, working for dignity, renouncing and denouncing all that is death-dealing, growing in truth and love and fidelity, and drawing others into this life-giving creative activity.

Notice that their model here is not one of self-emptying and self-depletion, but one of radiant overflow. We seek to be filled with a love that overflows and pours forth into the world around us. It is not what the self does at all; it is what God does, in and with us, in the measure that we open ourselves to the deepening movement of God within us and through us. Not only is this counsel one that liberates us from burnout and the delusion that we can do all things; it also frees us from the clutter of things that are not worthy of our attention, so that we can love with greater depth, intensity, and delight. As Iain Matthew so cogently explains:

> To step free from enslavement, we need a love which fills us at the point we thought the enslaving loves were filling us. To transcend our mediocrity, we need a love which touches us at the threshold of our fear. John presents a God whose love does that. Such is the conclusion to which 1 *Ascent* 13 leads: if our cravings and impulses are what normally inflame us, we need 'another greater inflaming by another better love, the love of [our] Bridegroom'—so, finding our 'fulfillment and strength' in this, we may have the strength 'easily' to stand free from any other.[40]

Clearly, this orientation to the wellspring of God's love is what Pope Francis has called the "interior impulse which encourages, motivates, nourishes and gives meaning to our individual and communal activity"[41] and that he enjoins us to recover, as a people in need of conversion to "a new and universal solidarity."[42]

---

of love—so much so that it seems consumed in the flame, which makes it leave itself and become wholly renewed and come into a new way of being, just like the phoenix that is burned and rises anew from the ashes."

40. Matthew, *Impact of God*, 49; cf. AMC I:14:2.
41. Pope Francis, *Joy of the Gospel*, par. 261.

For Teresa and John, this solidarity is learned, as Peter-Hans Kolvenbach once put it so saliently, "through contact, not concepts."[43] Their primary contact was an intimate friendship with Christ, discovered as they allowed Christ's own vulnerability to embolden them to be better friends. As Teresa puts it in her *Life*: "It seemed to me that I did better when I approached Christ in the places where I saw him more alone. For it seems to me that, being alone and afflicted, like a person in need, he would let me in. . . . In particular I found the place of his prayer in the Garden very helpful: that is where I went to keep him company."[44] Such experiences of prayer convinced Teresa of "the divine commitment to solidarity with us,"[45] and sensitized her to the incarnation as a reality of solidarity in which she, too, could live.

Teresa's example becomes a useful one, whether for a discursive meditative practice in which we imagine and enter into a consideration of a scene in Christ's life, or whether we engage more directly the need of the suffering Christ in others who are alone and vulnerable. Attending to Christ—responding, that is, to Christ's plea to "stay with me"—is emphatically not simply an internal practice. We live in a world in which people are continually trampled down, needing accompaniment, and to attend to Christ in that way is a critical prayer practice, as Teresa herself says:

> It benefits me little to be by myself and very recollected, making acts of devotion to God, proposing and promising to do wonders in God's service if, when I leave that space and an occasion to serve offers itself to me, I do everything the opposite.[46]

Friendship and constancy in vulnerability become a bridge to knowing the presence of God in the human community. Again, the idea is not

---

42. Cf. Pope Francis, *On Care for Our Common Home*, pars. 216 and 14.
43. Peter-Hans Kolvenbach, "The Service of Faith and the Promotion of Justice in American Jesuit Higher Education," Address at Santa Clara University, published in Faith, Justice and American Higher Education (2001).
44. L 9:4.
45. Iain Matthew, "St. Teresa: Witness to Christ's Resurrection;" paper delivered at conference entitled "Teresa of Avila 1515 to 2015: Mystical Theology and Spirituality in the Carmelite Tradition" at St Mary's University Twickenham, June 18–20, 2015; publication forthcoming.
46. IC VII:4:7. See also IC VII:4:6: "This is what prayer is for, my daughters, and this is what this spiritual marriage serves: from them both are always born good works."

choosing between contemplation and action, but to find the growing consistency and coherence between the two. For in attending to the presence of Christ by turns, in solitude and in engagement, we gain increasing clarity that we are, quite literally, *accompanied* in our daily life, even as our desire to accompany others faithfully grows within us.

As we have seen, one element of the legacy of Teresa and John's message is that it demonstrates the inherent coherence of contemplation and prophetic witness. To appreciate Teresa and John, especially as, together, they create a whole new movement of spiritual practice, is to recognize how a contemplative life takes form and shape in the world. Indeed, that taking form and shape is, in itself, a prophetic act, a unique witness to the reality that God can be incarnated in our midst as we grow into our partnership with God and bring it into the full range of our lives in the world and relationships with others. In theological terms, it is participation in the incarnation, and, as both clearly teach, radical solidarity with Christ gradually becomes the point of entry into the life of the Trinity. If Christ is the "living space opening up for us relationship with God,"[47] this is a relational way of life, an invitation to life in the Trinity:

> The paradigm that Teresa explores is how the fullness of union with God endows the soul with strength; over the course of repeated experiences of such union, the soul comes into its deepest potentiality, which is not of its own nature as an individual, but *is* within its growing nature as a partner of God; this is its potentiality-in-God and, as Teresa writes, "From this union comes its fortitude."[48]

The union that Teresa speaks of here is experienced, ultimately as an invitation into the vitality and dynamism of the Trinitarian God, as we saw at the end of her *Interior Castle*:

> And each day this soul is more amazed, for these Persons never seem to leave it, but it clearly beholds, that they are within it. In the extreme interior, in some place very deep within itself, the nature of which it doesn't know how to explain, because of a lack of learning, it perceives this divine company . . . in which it always remains.[49]

47. Iain Matthew, "St. Teresa: Witness to Christ's Resurrection."
48. *Entering*, 84. See IC VI:1:2.

This union gives us aspirations in love that we know are far beyond what we ourselves can generate. Through these aspirations, Teresa says, "the soul understands clearly that it is God who gives life to our soul. These aspirations come very, very often in such a living way that they can in no way be doubted."[50]

Both Teresa and John are deeply concerned about the kind of person one becomes, through relationship with God. This is not merely a moral question having to do with growth in virtue. Nor do Teresa and John frame their concerns in terms of "identity." They are far more concerned about the recovery of the image of God in us. Indeed, they would understand this process, I think, in terms of a "vivification" of that image. Teresa and John's God (and, I would hope, ours, too) is a living God, and therefore, a God who constantly gives new life, new possibility to all creation. God is a constant source, for them, of both identity and life—an identity that is "borrowed" or, better, *grown*, relationally, in us, over time, through the progression of our intimacy with God. Ultimately, this is an incarnational restoration—or as John puts it, it is the gradual but thorough "assimilation" of the God-presence in the human person.[51] There is (and probably will be) continuing disagreement over *what*, exactly, is "actualized" in this process and how to speak of the "self-realization" of the human person in consummated love-relation with God. However, there is great promise in communicating means of "actualizing" the relational self that constitutes the reality of the human person. When we know and understand ourselves as relational, and when that relationality is grounded in our relationship with God, we have the God-given capacity to actualize a genuine, living partnership with God that is, like the garden of John's *Spiritual Canticle*, constantly teeming with life, or, as Teresa put it above, "always birthing good works." Thus, the mystical life is an invitation to us to be active partners in the work of bringing new life to the human community. This partnership bears fruit very concretely—in imagination, in creativity, in seeing and implementing

---

49. IC VII:1:7. See above, pp. 68–9.
50. IC VII:2:6; cf. *Entering*, 117.
51. See, e.g., DN II:20:5.

possibilities—in all of what we typically associate with visionary leaders who move things from ideas into reality and who support and contribute to personal and social transformation.

Another critical application of this principle of transformation is necessary for life in our world today. If Teresa and John provide us with a way of moving toward the identity that God extends to us as God's beloved, they offer us trustworthy tools for identity formation in a time in which we are vulnerable to all kinds of false information about who we are, what we want, what we need, and where we are going. Perhaps the most hopeful application of Teresa and John's theology of transformation is its capacity to provide a viable path toward post-traumatic identity re-formation. The same tools that are capable of helping us form an identity in neutral terrain are capable of helping us form a new identity when the old one has been shattered by trauma. They provide legitimate categories for establishing what is truest and most reliable on the basis of what is rooted in dignity and incarnational presence. When life circumstances or human relations shatter our capacity to recognize that dignity, especially in ourselves, they offer us a programmatic way of re-gaining ownership of that dignity and claiming for ourselves and others an identity rooted in a love that constantly acknowledges and cherishes that dignity. The integrity of the divine–human partnership that Teresa and John teach is an integrity with the capacity to bind together the fragments not only of the self, but of brokennesses in the human community as they are seen and known in the light of the presence of God.

Teresa and John teach us that authentic theology is always and seeks always to be practical, to transform, to move things toward the greater good, toward the "perfection" of all things, not as perfect forms in and of themselves, but in some kind of mysterious communion in which each thing has its rightful place even as nothing is whole in and of itself. All is known in relationship, a relationship that constantly challenges and accompanies us in the work of becoming.

Teresa and John's legacy is the gift of accessibility. They make themselves radically accessible to us, as writers, spiritual guides, and companions. They make God accessible to us and teach us that we ourselves are desirable. They teach us that by opening ourselves and making ourselves accessible to the transforming love of God in ongoing and deepening ways, we are drawn into the love that gives life. Endowed with the capacity to love, each of us, no matter what our station, can be empowered in that love to enkindle love in others and rejoice in the fruits of new life.

Appendix: The Mystical Ladder
of Divine Love

(John of the Cross, *Dark Night of the Soul*, Book II, Chapters 19–20)

"For love is like a fire which always rises upwards
as though longing to be engulfed in its center."

The mystical ladder of divine love consists of ten steps.

Step 1: Lovesickness. "The first step of love makes the soul sick in an advantageous way." The bride [of the Song of Songs] speaks of this when she says: "I adjure you, daughters of Jerusalem, if you encounter my Beloved, tell him that I am lovesick." (Song of Songs 5:8) "Yet this sickness is not unto death but for the glory of God." In this state, we lose our appetite for all things except God. The state suggests a sharpened appetite and heightened sensitivity to what supports our love-relationship with God.[1] Because this is a space of deep longing without much experience in sustaining the desire of love, John says that it is not a space in which to linger. It purifies and prepares us to advance toward God. But it is uncomfortable and we do not dwell there, since we "languish" here.[2]

---

1. And is therefore consistent with the disposition of the person making Ignatius Loyola's Spiritual Exercises, especially in considering the Principle and Foundation of the Exercises (par. 23): "I want and I choose what better leads to God's deepening life in me."
2. Cf. Teresa, *Interior Castle*, II:1:2: "These rooms, in part, involve much more effort than do the first..."

Step 2: Seeking for God "unceasingly." Desire for God moves us to seek God more actively. The Bride in the Song of Songs is again invoked: "I shall rise up and seek the One whom my soul loves." (Song of Songs 3:1–2; see also Song of Songs 3:3–4) and "Seek the face of God always." (Ps. 104:4). Here, we look for our Beloved in all things. This is a place where deep yearnings are solidified. John writes: "In all its thoughts, the soul turns immediately to the Beloved; in all conversation and business it at once speaks about the Beloved; when eating, sleeping, keeping vigil or doing anything else, it centers all its care on the Beloved." This state is a remedy and "convalescence" to the languishing of the first step, and in this seeking the soul gains strength in love.

Step 3: Performing deeds of love. The third step prompts the soul to works of love and gives it fervor to move forward. In this fervor, the person thinks that all the works done for the Beloved are small and insignificant, in part because the desire to demonstrate love is so strong. The fire of love is now burning within, imparting strength in service. John uses the example of Jacob, who thought nothing of seven more years of service in order to be able to marry his beloved Rachel. (Gen. 29:20, 30) The soul may also experience sorrow or pain in feeling that he has not done enough for God.[3] Because the soul wants to do even more for God than what she can, she is freed here from vanity, presumption, and anything but sincere and devoted love. The soul also grows in solicitude, courage and strength.

Step 4: Increased devotion and the coalescence of greater energy to love. In this stage, the soul possesses even greater energy to love, so that "all its care is directed toward how it might give some pleasure to God and render service to God, even if that involves some cost." This step reflects a genuine love that is other-oriented, unconcerned

---

3. cf. Spiritual Exercises, par. 234: "God creates me out of love and desires nothing more than a return of love on my part. So much does God love me that even though I turn away and make little response, this Giver of all good gifts continues to be my Savior and Redeemer . . . If I were to respond as a reasonable person, what could I give in return to such a Lover?"

about self-interest.[4] Because this love is more genuine, the soul often experiences a sense of God's presence, giving it true delight in God. The effects of this step are to enkindle and enflame the soul further.

Step 5: Impatient desire and longing for God. "My soul longs and faints for the dwelling places of God." (Ps. 83:2) The very longing that the soul feels for God actually feeds the soul; now (as opposed to step 1) the soul can sustain this longing and benefit from it, for it has experienced God (step 4) and has greater confidence that its longing will be assuaged.

Step 6: Running swiftly toward God and experiencing God's touches. The soul is able to "run swiftly without fainting" because it has deep hope in God at this stage. "The saints who hope in God shall renew their strength. They shall take wings like the eagle and shall fly and not faint." (Isa. 40:31). John also cites Ps. 41:2: "As the hart desires the waters, so does my soul desire You, my God," saying that the deer, when thirsty, "races toward the water." This fervor imparts both strength and speed. "The reason for the swiftness of love on this step is that the soul's charity is now highly increased and almost completely purified. "I have run the way of Your commandments when You have enlarged my heart."[5]

Step 7: Ardent boldness in love. In this stage, God's favors give the soul great boldness in love and it loses any shame regarding love. It is this kind of love that "believes all things, hopes all things, endures all things." (1 Cor. 13:7) "These souls obtain from God what they ask from God with pleasure," John says, and he cites the bride's entreaty at the outset of the Song of Songs: "Let him kiss me with the kiss of his mouth." (Song of Songs 1:1) The soul's boldness is preceded by some indication from God of divine favor, which increases the soul's

---

4. Bernard of Clairvaux would call this the third stage of his four stages of love (*On Loving God*), in which a person begins to love God for God's sake (and not for what God can do for us).
5. Cf. Teresa, *Interior Castle*, fourth dwelling places, esp. IV:2:5–6.

confidence in the love of God. One of the spiritual gifts here is true confidence, even assuredness about God's love.

Step 8: Adherence to God. In this step, the soul begins to "cling" to God: "The eighth step of love impels the soul to lay hold of the Beloved without letting go, as the bride proclaims: 'I found the One whom my soul loves; Whom I held and did not let go." (Song of Songs 3:4) However, the soul lacks experience in sustaining union, and this "clinging" or "cleaving" is temporary, not continual. "If one were to remain on this step," John says, "a certain glory would be possessed in this life." Daniel, the "man of desires," was allowed, even told, to "remain on this step," because of his great desire.

Step 9: A love that causes the soul to "burn gently." "The Holy Spirit produces this gentle and delightful ardor" through the soul's union with God. This is the "perfection" of love in this life. John says: "We cannot speak of the goods and riches of God enjoyed at this stage because even were we to write many books about them, the greater part would remain unsaid."

Step 10: Assimilation into God "because of the clear vision of God that the soul possesses" at this stage. "Blessed are the pure of heart for they shall see God." (Matt. 5:8) This vision of God gives the soul a likeness to God and even a participation in God. John says it is not experienced in this life.

Bibliography

Primary Sources

The Collected Works of St. John of the Cross, edited by Kieran Kavanaugh, O.C.D., and Otilio Rodriguez, O.C.D. Washington, DC: Institute of Carmelite Studies, 1979.

Francis. *Joy of the Gospel*. Washington, DC: United States Conference of Catholic Bishops, 2013.

Kolvenbach, Peter-Hans. "The Service of Faith and the Promotion of Justice in American Jesuit Higher Education." Address at Santa Clara University, published in Faith, Justice and American Higher Education, 2001.

Osuna, Francisco de. *The Third Spiritual Alphabet*, trans. Mary Giles. New York: Paulist, 1981.

San Bartolomé, Ana de. *Autobiography and Other Writings*, translated by Darcy Donahue. Chicago: University of Chicago Press, 2008.

Santa Maria, Francisco de. *Reforma de los Descalzos de Nuestra Señora del Carmen de la primitiva observancia*. Madrid, 1644.

Secondary Sources

Ahlgren, Gillian. "Negotiating Sanctity: Holy Women in Sixteenth-Century Spain," *Church History* vol. 64, no. 3 (September, 1995): 373–88.

____. "Teresa of Avila" in *The Reformation Theologians*, edited by Carter Lindberg. Oxford: Blackwell, 2002.

Andrés, Melquíades. *La teología española en al siglo XVI* vols. 1 and 2. Madrid: Biblioteca de Autores Cristianos, 1976.

Arenal, Electa and Stacey Schlau. *Untold Sisters: Hispanic Nuns in Their Own Works.* Albuquerque: University of New Mexico Press, 1989.

Bilinkoff, Jodi. "Teresa of Avila: Woman with a Mission" in *A Linking of Heaven and Earth: Studies in Religious and Cultural History in Honor of Carlos M. N. Eire,* edited by Emily Michelson, Scott K. Taylor, and Mary Noll Venables. Burlington, VT: Ashgate, 2013.

____. "Touched by Teresa: Readers and their Responses, 1588–1750" in *The Heirs of St. Teresa: Defenders and Disseminators of the Founding Mother's Legacy,* edited by Christopher Wilson. Washington, DC: Institute of Carmelite Studies, 2006.

Cortes, Narciso Alonso. "Pleitos de los Cepeda" in *Boletín de la Real Academia Española* 25 (1946): 85–110.

Dombrowski, Daniel. *St. John of the Cross: An Appreciation.* Albany, NY: SUNY Press, 1992.

Doohan, Leonard. *The Contemporary Challenge of John of the Cross: An Introduction to His Life and Teaching.* Washington, DC: Institute of Carmelite Studies, 1995.

Egido, Teófanes. *El linaje judeoconverso de Santa Teresa: pleito de hidalguía de los Cepeda.* Madrid: Editorial de Espiritualidad, 1986.

____. "La Familia judía de Santa Teresa," *Studia Zamorensia* 3 (1982): 449–79.

____, ed. *Perfil histórico de Santa Teresa.* Madrid: Editorial de Espiritualidad, 1981.

Garcia de la Concha, Victor. *El arte literario de Santa Teresa.* Barcelona: Ariel, 1978.

Hamilton, Alastair. *Heresy and Mysticism in Sixteenth-Century Spain.* Cambridge: James Clarke and Co., 1992.

Harbison, Robert. *Reflections on Baroque.* Chicago: University of Chicago, 2000.

Hardy, Richard P. *John of the Cross: Man and Mystic.* Boston, MA: Pauline Books, 2004.

Herrera, Clara A. "Influences of St. Catherine of Siena and St. Teresa of Avila on the Columbian Nun Jerónima Nava y Saavedra" in *A New Companion to Hispanic Mysticism,* edited by Hilaire Kelendorf. Leiden: Brill, 2010.

Howells, Edward. *John of the Cross and Teresa of Avila: Mystical Knowing and Selfhood.* New York: Crossroad, 2002.

Kavanaugh, Kieran. *John of the Cross: Doctor of Light and Love*. New York: Crossroad, 1999.

LaCugna, Catherine Mowry. *God for Us: The Trinity and Christian Life*. New York: Harper Collins, 1991.

Llamas, Enrique. *Santa Teresa y la Inquisición Española*. Madrid: Editorial de Espiritualidad, 1972.

Luti, J. Mary. *Teresa of Avila's Way*. Collegeville, MN: Liturgical, 1991.

Martin, Dennis D. *Carthusian Spirituality: The Writings of Hugh of Balma and Guigo de Ponte*. Mahwah, NY: Paulist, 1997.

Matthew, Iain. *Impact of God*. London: Hodder and Stoughton, 1995.

____. "St. Teresa: Witness to Christ's Resurrection." Paper delivered at conference entitled "Teresa of Avila 1515 to 2015: Mystical Theology and Spirituality in the Carmelite Tradition" at St Mary's University Twickenham, June 18–20, 2015; publication forthcoming.

McIntosh, Mark. *Mystical Theology: The Integrity of Spirituality and Theology*. Malden, MA: Blackwell, 1998.

Merton, Thomas. *Ascent to Truth*. New York: Harcourt Brace, 1951.

Mujica, Barbara. *Teresa of Ávila: Lettered Woman*. Nashville: Vanderbilt University Press, 2009.

Muto, Susan. *John of the Cross for Today: The Dark Night*. Notre Dame, IN: Ave Maria, 1994.

Nicolás, Adolfo. "Depth, Universality, and Learned Ministry: Challenges to Jesuit Higher Education Today" in *Santa Clara Magazine*, Winter 2010.

Pablo Maroto, Daniel de. *Santa Teresa de Jesús: Nueva Biografía (Escritora, fundadora, maestra)*. Madrid: Editorial de Espiritualidad, 2014.

____. *Ser y misión del Carmelo Teresiano: Historia de un carisma*. Madrid: Editorial de Espiritualidad, 2010.

Payne, Steven, ed. *John of the Cross: Conferences and Essays by Members of the Institute of Carmelite Studies and Others*. Washington, DC: Institute of Carmelite Studies, 1992.

Pinto Crespo, Virgilio. *Inquisición y control ideológico en la España del siglo XVI*. Barcelona: Ariel, 1983.

Rossi, Rosa. *Teresa de Avila: Biografía de una escritora*, translated by Marieta Gargategli. Barcelona: ICARIA, 1984.

Ruiz, F. *God Speaks in the Night: The Life, Times, and Teaching of St. John of the Cross.* Washington, DC: Institute of Carmelite Studies, 1991.

Sáinz Rodriguez, Pedro. *La siembra mística del Cardenal Cisneros y las reformas en la Iglesia.* Madrid: Fundación Universitaria Española, 1979.

San Joaquin, Antonio de, *Año teresiano, diario histórico, panegyrico moral, en que se discubren las virtudes, sucesos y maravaillas de la seráphica y mistica Doctora de la Iglesia Santa Teresa de Jesús.* Madrid, 1733–69.

Seris, Homero. "Nueva geneología de Santa Teresa" in *Nueva Revista de Filología Hispànica* 10 (1965): 363–84.

Sicroff, Albert A. *Los Estatutos de Limpieza de Sangre: controversias entre los siglos XV y XVII.* Madrid: Taurus, 1985.

Slattery, Peter, ed. *St. John of the Cross: A Spirituality of Substance.* New York: Alba House, 1994.

Smet, Joachim. *The Carmelites: A History of the Brothers of Our Lady of Mount Carmel,* 5 vols. Darien, IL: The Carmelite Press, 1988.

Steggink, Otger. "Dos corrientes de reforma en al Carmelo español del siglo XVI: La observancia y la descalcez, frente a la 'Reforma del rey,' "*Aspectos históricos,* 117–42.

_____. "Arraigo carmelitano de Santa Teresa" in *The Land of Carmel: Essays in Honor of Joachim Smet,* edited by Paul Chandler and Keith J. Egan. Rome: Institutum Carmelitanum, 1991.

Stopp, Elizabeth. *A Man to Heal Differences: Essays and Talks on St. Francis de Sales.* Philadelphia: St. Joseph's University, 1997.

Thompson, Colin. *John of the Cross: Songs in the Night.* Washington, DC: The Catholic University of America, 2003.

Tyler, Peter. *The Return to the Mystical: Ludwig Wittgenstein, Teresa of Avila, and the Christian Mystical Tradition.* New York: Continuum, 2011.

_____. *Saint John of the Cross.* New York: Continuum, 2010.

_____. *Teresa of Avila: Doctor of the Soul.* New York: Continuum, 2014.

Turner, Denys. *Eros and Allegory: Medieval Exegesis of the Song of Songs.* Kalamazoo, MI: Cistercian Publications, 1995.

Vermeylen, Alphonse. *Sainte Thérèse en France au XVIIe siècle 1600-1660.* Louvain: Publications Universitaires, 1958.

Villanueva, Francisco Marquez. "Santa Teresa y el linaje" in *Espiritualidad y literatura en el siglo XVI*. Madrid: Alfaguera, 1968.

Weber, Alison. *Book for the Hour of Recreation*. Chicago: University of Chicago, 2002.

____. "María de San José: Saint Teresa's Difficult Daughter" in Christopher Wilson, *The Heirs of St. Teresa of Avila*, 1–20.

____. "Spiritual Administration: Gender and Discernment in the Carmelite Reform" in *Sixteenth Century Studies* 31(1) Spring 2000:123–46.

____. *Teresa of Avila and the Rhetoric of Femininity*. Princeton: Princeton University, 1991.

Wilson, Christopher C. *The Heirs of St. Teresa: Defenders and Disseminators of the Founding Mother's Legacy*. Washington, DC: Institute of Carmelite Studies, 2006.

Wyhe, Cordula van. "The Teresian Mystic Life and its Visual Representation in the Low Countries" in *Female Monasticism in Early Modern Europe*, edited by Cordula van Wyhe. Burlington, VT: Ashgate, 2008.

Index of Names and Places

Index of Subjects

Index of Scripture